HOW TO MAKE A
ONESIE

HOW TO MAKE A ONESIE

Janelle Fischer

Contents

Introduction

'I was sewing when sewing wasn't cool'.
I love that saying, it describes me perfectly.
My mum used to keep her sewing machine set
up in her walk-in wardrobe. I was fascinated by
the idea that if she went into the wardrobe and
couldn't find something to wear then she could
just sit down and make it!

Sadly for my mother, by the tender age of
eight I had taken over her small sewing space
and she now had to get in line to use her
sewing machine and her wardrobe! My mum
was taught to sew by her mother. This used
to be the sewing cycle. Mums taught their
daughters and then those daughters went on
to teach their daughters. But this cycle gave
way when clothing in the stores became much
cheaper than sewing something yourself. So the
cycle ended.

I was, however, one of the exceptions.
I begged my mum to show me the basics and
somehow it just all made sense. By high school
I was sewing formal dresses (puffy sleeves and
all) while my friends were struggling with a
pillowcase.

I guess it was inevitable that sewing would
become my career and after many years
working in almost every area of the fashion
industry, I have returned to teaching. Many of
my students are children and the feedback that
I receive from their parents is how wonderful it
is to see the resurrection of this beautiful craft.

Hopefully the sewing cycle will return with this new generation of students.

When you can sew you often find yourself making some very unusual items. Some time ago, before onesies were readily available, my children began showing me pictures of very cute and cosy, all-in-one, character jump suits. 'Can you make one of these for me, Mum?' My first attempt was a cow. At that time it was hard to locate the fabric so I used a fur blanket; my daughter was thrilled but somewhat over warm most of the time! Soon enough onesies became a hugely popular trend for adults and children alike, and more suitable fabrics began to be available.

Onesies have now become a standard addition to most children's wardrobes. I have seen them worn to school discos, put on after swimming lessons, and even worn to the movies. Children love wearing them, they are amazingly comfortable and the character design possibilities are truly endless.

I hope this book will not only guide you through the simple steps to making a onesie but also offer ideas and inspiration for creating a fun and forever-loved character. Don't be afraid to mix it up a bit, change fabric colours or even design your own character. With the wide variety of styles, and the templates and patterns included in this book, you should be able to create just about any style imaginable.

I hope you enjoy your journey into the magical land of onesies. Your sewing room may end up covered in fluff but your children will love watching the character emerge. They may even want to add their own special touches. One of the most enjoyable parts of creating this book has been involving my children in the designs. They have offered fantastic feedback to my never ending questions, 'Does this tail look right?' 'Are these eyes too big?' The end result does not need to be perfect, and in some ways those little imperfections will be what makes your onesie all the more special.

Janelle Fischer

Fabric and Yardage

The first stage of making a onesie is selecting the right amount of fabric. I have divided the designs in this book into two versions, A and B, which will make it easier to adapt the templates and follow the design instructions. Version A is for the basic style onesie, while Version B has a front insert and a two-piece hood.

Suggested fabrics

Onesies are generally made from knitted fleece fabrics that are typically made from polyester. Fleece fabrics have a tendency to shrink after washing, therefore it is recommended to pre-wash all fabrics before cutting out the pattern. For the designs in this book I have used a variety of fleece fabric brands such as Minky, Coral and Polar. However, do not limit yourself; the leopard in this book was made from a lightweight throw! Due to the loose, easy fit of a onesie it could be made in just about any fabric. You could even consider a woven fabric if the print suited your project. Knitted fabrics are usually more comfortable, however, and the cuffs should always be made from a knit fabric.

Fleece fabric has a tendency to be thick in areas where seams overlap, which can become a problem when sewing. To solve this problem I suggest you use a walking foot attachment on your sewing machine whenever possible, and consider choosing a lighter weight fabric for the hood linings.

All onesies in this book are made using one of two sets of templates, which are provided.

Ironing

Avoid using the iron altogether on fleece fabrics. The iron will flatten the pile and leave a shiny mark, and in some cases could even melt the material. Fleece fabrics adapt well and should not need pressing after sewing. In cases where the iron cannot be avoided, such as when using a fusible web, it is recommended you use a pressing cloth, and set the iron to the 'synthetic' setting.

Needles

When sewing with knitted fabrics it is recommended to use ballpoint or stretch needles.

Fabric quantities

You need to purchase main and ribbing fabric for making a onesie. Use the tables below for all the onesie projects in this book.

Measurements for version A

Main fabric				Ribbing fabric				Buttons 1.6 cm (5/8 inch)	
Age/size	metres	yards		Age/size	cm	inches		age/size	quantity
2	1.3	1½		2	15	6		2	4
4	1.5	1.7		4	15	6		4	5
6	1.6	1.8		6	15	6		6	5
8	1.8	2		8	15	6		8	6
10	1.9	2.1		10	15	6		10	6

Measurements for version B

Main fabric			Contrast fabric			Rib fabric			Buttons 1.6 cm (5/8 in)	
Age/size	m	yds	Age/size	cm	in	Age/size	cm	in	Age/size	quantity
2	1.3	1½	2	60	24	2	15	6	2	4
4	1.5	1.7	4	65	26	4	15	6	4	5
6	1.6	1.8	6	70	28	6	15	6	6	5
8	1.8	2	8	75	30	8	15	6	8	6
10	1.9	2.1	10	80	32	10	15	6	10	6

Second contrast fabric

Some styles require additional contrast fabrics. Refer to the instruction sheet for that specific style for this information, but as a general rule all sizes need 56 cm/22 inches.

The Patterns

The two master patterns you will need to make the styles in this book can be found at the back of the book. Use Version A for the basic style onesie. Use Version B for those with a front insert and a two-piece hood. Each style advises which to use.

   The pattern will need to be enlarged onto A3 paper with a photocopier to the percentage indicated and then joined together to create a full-size pattern.

   Trace the appropriately-sized pattern pieces for your chosen style.

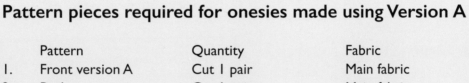

Pattern pieces required for onesies made using Version A

	Pattern	Quantity	Fabric
1.	Front version A	Cut 1 pair	Main fabric
2.	Back	Cut 1 pair	Main fabric
3.	Sleeve	Cut 1 pair	Main fabric
4.	Hood version A	Cut 1 pair	Main fabric
5.	Sleeve band	Cut 1 pair	Ribbing
6.	Leg band	Cut 1 pair	Ribbing

Pattern pieces required for onesies made using Version B

	Pattern	Quantity	Fabric
1.	Front version B	Cut 1 pair	Main fabric
2.	Front insert	Cut 1 pair	Contrast fabric
3.	Back	Cut 1 pair	Main fabric
4.	Sleeve	Cut 1 pair	Main fabric
5.	Back hood	Cut 1 pair	Main fabric and lining
6.	Front hood	Cut 1	Main fabric and lining
7.	Sleeve band	Cut 1 pair	Ribbing
8.	Leg band	Cut 1 pair	Ribbing

Version A:

The Basic Onesie

This basic pattern is ideal for everyday onesies, for which you can use a whole range of fabrics to create many and varied results. This version works especially well if you are using a patterned fabric that needs no enhancements.

Cutting

The fabric requirements are listed in the measurement charts on page 9. Use all the pattern pieces from Version A.

Assembly

All the seam allowances are 1.5 cm/5/8 inch.
Once you have cut out all of the pattern pieces, simply follow the assembly instructions for Version A, Steps 1–11.

Cutting Version A

Many fleece fabrics have a nap or a one-way design. For this reason is it recommended to cut all the pieces in the same direction.

Main fabric

All the pattern pieces for Version A – front, back, sleeve and hood specify to 'cut 1 pair'. Fold the fabric in half lengthwise so all patterns have their length running with the length of the fabric. Position these pieces onto the fabric with the grain line parallel to the selvage of the fabric. Pin pieces into place, then carefully cut around all pattern pieces.

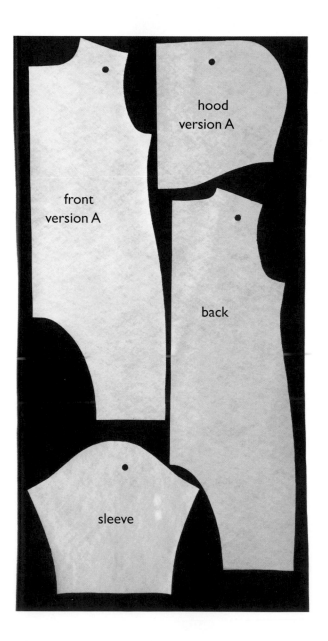

Ribbing

The leg band and sleeve band pattern pieces are 'cut
1 pair'. To achieve this, place these pieces on a double
layer of fabric with the grain-line on the
pattern parallel to the selvage of the
fabric. Carefully cut around all pattern
pieces. Ribbing fabric has a large amount
of stretch and is therefore ideal for areas
such as cuffs where stretch and return
is required.

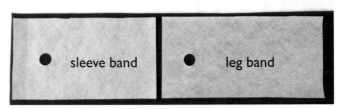

Cutting

Fleece fabric can be thick so a good sharp pair
of scissors is recommended. If you are having
trouble, try only cutting one layer at a time.
When cutting in a single layer be mindful to flip
the pattern pieces for the second cut therefore
still resulting in a pair.

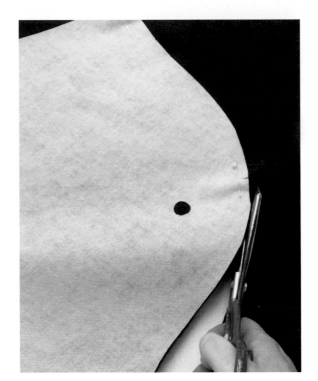

Getting the size right

If your child is tall for their
age then be sure to add
some extra length to the
legs before cutting out
the pattern.

Assembling Version A

All the seam allowances are 1.5 cm/⁵⁄₈ inch unless otherwise stated, and back tack (reverse stitch) is required at the start and finish. Finish all the seams after sewing with a serger, an overlocker or a zig zag stitch.

1. Centre back seam (right)

Place the pair of back pieces with right sides together. Pin, sew and serge/overlock the centre back seam from the neck edge to the crotch.

2. Shoulder seams (above)

With right sides together, pin, sew and serge/overlock the front and back pieces at the shoulder seams.

3. Hood seam (right)

With right sides together, pin the curved edge of the hood pieces, then sew and serge/overlock.

4. Attaching the hood (left)

With right sides together pin and sew the lower edge of the hood to the neck line. Match the centre back seams and line up the front edge of the hood with the centre front of the body. The notch on the hood should also match to the shoulder seam. Finish the edge with serge/overlock.

5. Inserting the sleeves (left)

With right sides together pin then sew the sleeves to the armholes. Match the notch on the sleeve to the shoulder seam join. Finish the edge with serge/overlock.

6. Front facing (right)

Serge/overlock the centre front edges, including the hood area. Fold the finished front edge 2.5 cm/1 inch towards the under-side. Stitch in place close to the previously serged/overlocked line.

7. Side seams (left)

With right sides together, pin, sew and serge/overlock the side seams. Begin at the sleeve opening and continue through the underarm join to the leg opening.

8. Inside leg seam (above right)

Overlap the front facings at the crotch by 2.5 cm/1 inch. As a general rule, male clothing wraps left over right, while female clothing wraps right over left. Secure in place with a baste.

Sew the front and back together along the inside leg seam. Start sewing at the ankle of one leg and continue across the crotch to finish at the other ankle. Finish the edge with serge/overlock.

9. Attaching the ribbing (below and following page, top)

With right sides together sew the two shorter edges of the ribbing together to form a circular piece. This process is repeated four times, once for each sleeve cuff and once for each leg cuff. Fold the tube in half with wrong sides together, matching the raw edges to form the cuff.

The ribbing is smaller than the sleeve opening to give a snug fit, and so needs to be stretched while sewing. To ensure the ribbing is stretched evenly, divide it into four equal sections, marking each quarter with a pin. Repeat the same quartering process on the opening of the sleeve/leg. Place the ribbing onto the sleeve/leg opening with right sides together, matching each quartered section. Sew the ribbing to the opening, gently stretching the ribbing in each quarter to match. Finish the edge with serge/overlock.

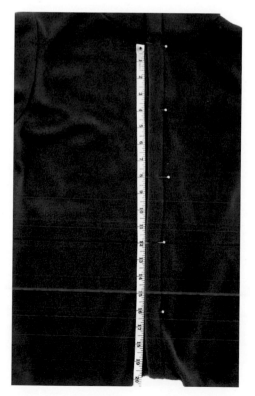

10. Making buttonholes
(left and overleaf, top)

Buttonholes are created on the front top facing, and buttons are sewn to the front under facing. Position the first buttonhole at the neckline and the last buttonhole approximately 10 cm/4 inches up from the crotch seam. Position the remaining buttonholes evenly spaced between the first and last. The number of buttonholes will depend on the size of the onesie you are making. Refer to the Fabric and Yardage guide on pages 8–9 to determine the amount of buttons required.

  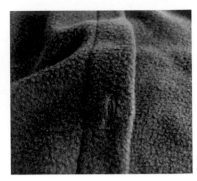

Each brand of sewing machine will differ slightly in buttonhole application. Please refer to the manufacturer's manual for details. Sew the buttonholes, then carefully slice them open using a stitch unpick.

11. Sewing on buttons (below)

Determine the button positions by making a chalk mark through the buttonholes onto the under facing.
Buttons can be sewn on by hand or by using the sewing machine. If using the sewing machine, remove the presser foot, set the machine to zig zag and reduce the stitch length to zero.

Before sewing the button, be sure to test that the zig zag width matches the width between the holes on the button. It is safest to use the hand wheel initially. This may seem quicker than hand sewing but take care; many needles have been broken with this method!

 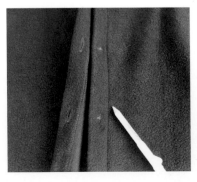 

Version B:

The Character Onesie

This pattern is ideal for all the character onesies, for which you can use a whole range of fabrics to create many and varied results.

Cutting

The fabric requirements are listed in the measurement charts on pages 8–9. Use all the pattern pieces from version B plus the additional template pieces as listed in the individual characters cutting instructions.

Assembly

All the seam allowances are 1.5cm/⁵/₈ in.

Once your have cut out all the pattern pieces, refer to the individual character for assembly instructions.

Getting the size right

If your child is tall for their age then be sure to add some extra length to the legs before cutting out the pattern.

Cutting Version B

Many fleece fabrics have a nap or a one-way design. For this reason is it recommended to cut the pieces in the same the direction.

Some styles from Version B have the hood lined in a contrasting fabric, while others have the hood lined in the main fabric. The following instructions are for the contrasting hood liner. If the style you are making has the hood lined in the main fabric then cut two pairs of hood back and one pair of hood front in the main fabric instead of the contrast fabric.

Due to the thickness of fleece fabric, the Version B hood, with its multiple layers of fabric, can become very bulky. This can make sewing it to the neckline difficult. If possible choose an alternative lighter-weight jersey fabric for the lining pieces.

Main fabric

Fold the fabric in half lengthwise and, place the pieces on the fabric with the grain-line parallel to the selvage of the fabric. Cut one pair of front, back, sleeve and back hood pieces. Cut one front hood.

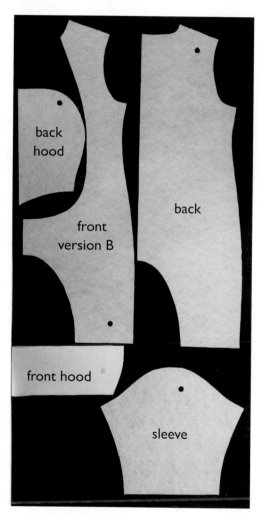

Contrast fabric

Cut one pair of front insert and back hood. Cut one front hood. These pieces also need to be placed on the fabric with the grain parallel to the selvage of the fabric.

Ribbing

The leg band and sleeve band pattern pieces are 'cut 1 pair'. To achieve this, place these pieces on a double layer of fabric with the grain-line on the pattern parallel to the selvage of the fabric.

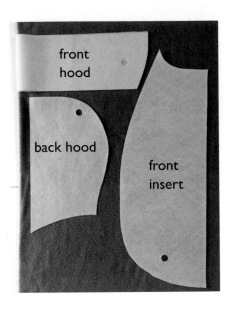

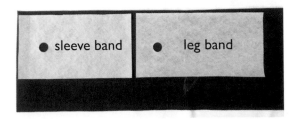

Cutting

Fleece fabric can be thick so a good sharp pair of scissors is recommended. If you are having trouble, try only cutting one layer at a time. when cutting in a single layer be mindful to flip the pattern pieces for the second cut therefore still resulting in a pair.

Assembling Version B

Version B onesies are constructed in a similar order as Version A, with the addition of the steps listed below. These steps will be referred to while following the instruction page from the specific onesie.

1. Front insert

With right sides together pin, sew and serge/overlock one of the front insert pieces to one of the front pieces. Repeat for the other side. Be careful with the curve on the front insert piece, as it may have stretched slightly after cutting and need some easing to fit into the curve on the front piece.

2. Hood assembly

With right sides together, pin and sew the curved edge of the back hood pieces. This seam will not need to be serged/overlocked as the hood will be lined.

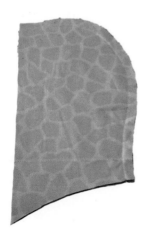

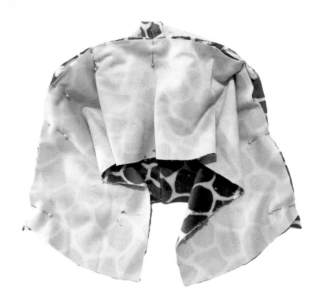

With right sides together pin and sew the front hood to the back hood. Follow the notches marked on the pattern to ensure the correct sides are sewn together.

Repeat this process for the lining.

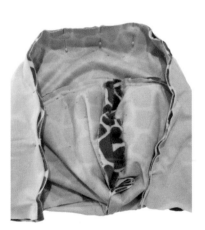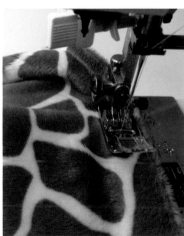

3. Sew the hood to the lining

With right sides together pin and sew the long edge of the front hood main fabric to the front hood lining fabric. Turn the hood to the right side. Topstitch along this edge to stop the lining from rolling out of place.

Run a basting stitch around the hood and lining, at the neckline edge. Securing these two edges together makes it is easier to sew the hood pieces to the body in the next step.

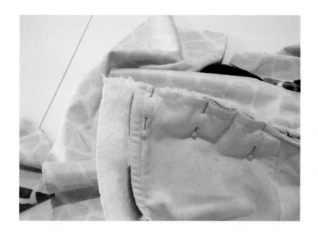 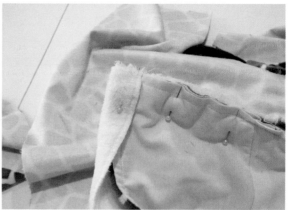

4. Sewing the hood to the body

Serge/overlock the two centre front edges. With right sides together pin the hood to the neckline, matching the centre back seams. The edge of the hood should be positioned 2.5 cm/1 inch in from the front edge on either side. Fold this 2.5 cm/1 inch of extra fabric back onto the neckline, encasing the hood, and pin in place. Sew around the neckline through all thicknesses, and finish the edge by serging.

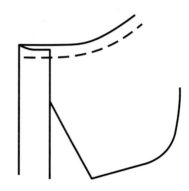

5. Sew front facing

Fold the finished front edge 2.5 cm/1 inch towards the under-side. Stitch in place close to the previously serged line.

The Characters

Dog

This cosy Dog onesie was the first design that I created for the book. I fell in love with him as he emerged, and I began to visualize how my other little projects were going to develop. Maybe this will be your very first furry friend too.

Cutting

The fabric requirements for this onesie are listed in the measurement chart on pages 8–9. Use the pattern pieces from Version B. You will also need these pieces from the Dog template page:

Ears:	Cut 1 pair from the main fabric and 1 pair from contrast fabric.
Outer eye:	Cut 1 pair from white felt.
Pupil:	Cut 1 pair from black felt.
Outer Nose:	Cut 1 from brown felt.
Inner Nose:	Cut 1 from black felt.
Tongue:	Cut 1 from red felt.
Tail:	Cut 1 piece 50 x 10 cm/ 20 x 4 inches from main fabric.

Cut the front insert and inside hood pieces from contrast fabric.

Assembly

All the seam allowances are 1.5 cm/⁵/₈ inch.

1. With right sides together, fold the tail in half lengthwise and sew the raw edges together. Leave one short end open. To achieve a curved end to the tail, finish one end with a curved stitch line. Trim the seam allowance to 6 mm/¹/₄ inch on the curved end. Turn the tail through to the right side.

2. Baste the tail to the right side of the centre back seam, positioning it 23 cm/9 inches up from the crotch.

3. For the centre back seam follow the assembly instructions for Version A, Step 1. For the front insert, follow the assembly instructions for Version B, Step 1. For the shoulder seams, follow the assembly instructions for Version A, Step 2.

4. Place one main fabric and one contrast fabric ear right sides together then pin and sew around the curved edge. Leave the straight edge open. Trim the seam to 6 mm/¹/₄ inch, and turn right side out. Make another ear. Baste a 1.5 cm/⁵/₈ inch-wide tuck into the base of each ear.

5. To assemble the hood, with right sides together, pin and sew the curved edge of the back hood pieces. This seam will not need to be serged/overlocked as the hood is lined. Baste the ears to the top of the hood back piece, 15 cm/6 inches apart, and level with each other, on each side of the centre hood seam.

6. With right sides together, pin and sew the front hood to the back hood. Follow the notches marked on the pattern to ensure the correct edges are sewn together. Repeat the hood assembly, without the ears, for the lining.

7. To create the face, attach the pre-cut template pieces to the front hood using a zig zag stitch set on a short stitch length. Work in the following order:
*   Stitch the pupil onto the eye.
*   Stitch the eyes onto the front hood, evenly positioned on each side of the centre.
*   Stitch the inner nose onto the outer nose.
*   Stitch the outer nose onto the face, centred and overlapping the eyes slightly.
*   Baste the tongue to the centre front of the hood.

8. Sew the hood and lining together following the assembly instructions for Version B, Step 3.
    Sew the hood to the body following the assembly instructions for Version B, Step 4.

9. Sew the front facing following the assembly instructions for Version B, Step 5. To insert the sleeves, follow the assembly instructions for Version A, Step 5.

10. Follow Steps 7–11 from the assembly instructions for Version A to finish the seams, attach the ribbing and create the buttonholes.

Cat

This cool Cat Onesie was created for all the cat lovers out there. The eyes may be a bit sly but I think, in this, the kids will look just purrrfect.

Cutting

The fabric requirements for this onesie are listed in the measurement chart on pages 8–9. Use the pattern pieces from Version B, together with these additional pieces from the Cat template page:

Ears:	Cut 1 pair from main fabric and 1 pair from contrast fabric.
Eyes:	Cut 1 pair from yellow felt.
Pupil:	Cut 1 pair from black felt.
Nose:	Cut 1 from white felt.
Tail:	Cut 1 from main fabric 50 x 10 cm/ 20 x 4 inches.

Cut the front insert and inside hood pieces in contrast fabric.

Assembly

All the seam allowances are 1.5 cm/⅝ inch.

1. With right sides together, fold the tail in half lengthwise and sew the raw edges together. Leave one end open. To achieve a curved end to the tail, finish one end with a curved stitch line. Trim the seam allowance back to 6 mm/¼ inch on the curved end. Turn the tail through to the right side.

fold

2. Baste the tail to the right side of the centre back seam, positioning it 23 cm/9 inches up from the crotch. For the centre back seam, follow the assembly instructions for Version A, Step 1.

3. For the front insert, follow the assembly instructions for Version B, Step 1. For the shoulder seams follow the assembly instructions for Version A, Step 2.

4. Place one main fabric and one contrast fabric ear right sides together. Pin and sew around the curved edge, leaving the straight edge open. Trim the seam to 6 mm/¼ inch and turn right side out. Make another ear.

5. To assemble the hood, with right sides together, pin and sew the curved edge of the back hood pieces. This seam will not need to be serged/overlocked as the hood is lined. Baste the ears in place to the top of the hood back piece, 7.5 cm/3 inches apart and evenly placed on each side of the centre hood seam.

6.   With right sides together, pin and sew the front hood to the back hood. Follow the notches marked on the pattern to ensure the correct edges are sewn together. Repeat the hood assembly for the lining without including the ears.

7.   To create the face, attach the pre-cut template pieces to the front hood using a zig zag stitch set on a short stitch length. Attach the pieces in the following order:
- Stitch the pupil onto the eye.
- Stitch the eyes onto the front hood, evenly positioned apart from the centre.
- Stitch the nose under the eyes.
- Use a decorative stitch under the nose to create the mouth.

8.   Sew the hood and the lining together, referring to the assembly instructions for version B and following Step 3. Sew the hood to the body, following the assembly instructions for version B, Step 4.

9.   Sew the front facing, following the assembly instructions for version B, Step 5. Insert the sleeves, following the assembly instructions for version A, Step 5.

10. Follow Steps 7–11 from the assembly instructions for version A to finish the seams, attach the ribbing and create the buttonholes.

Tiger

Be warned, after creating this onesie your sewing room will be covered in fluff, but it will all be worth it, as your little one will roar in this fabulous Tiger onesie.

Cutting

The fabric requirements for this onesie are listed in the measurement chart on pages 8–9. Use the pattern pieces from version B together with these additional pieces from the Tiger template page:

Ears: Cut 1 pair from main fabric and one
          pair from second contrast fabric
Tail: Cut 1 piece 50 x 10 cm/20 x 4 inches
          from the main fabric

Cut the front insert in contrast fabric (white), cut the inside hood pieces and inside ears from a second contrast fabric (brown). If possible, choose a lighter weight fabric to avoid bulk at the neck seam.

39

Assembly

All the seam allowances are 1.5 cm/⁵⁄₈ inch.

1. With right sides together, fold the tail in half lengthwise and sew the raw edges together. Leave one end open. To achieve a curved end to the tail, finish one end with a curved stitch line. Trim the seam allowance to 6 mm/¹⁄₄ inch on the curved end. Turn the tail through to the right side.

fold

2. Position the tail on the right side of the centre back seam, 23 cm/9 inches up from the crotch, and baste in place.

3. For the centre back seam, follow the assembly instructions for version A, Step 1. For the front insert follow the assembly instructions for version B, Step 1. For the shoulder seams, refer to the assembly instructions for version A, following Step 2.

4. Place one ear from the main fabric and one from the contrast fabric with right sides together, then pin and sew around the curved edge. Leave the straight edge open. Trim the seam to 6 mm/¹⁄₄ inch and turn to the right side. Baste a 1.5 cm/⁵⁄₈ inch-wide pleat into the base of the ear.

Creating a face

As the main fabric is patterned I have not created a face. However, if you wish to add eyes or a nose then refer to 'Create the Face' section from another similar design.

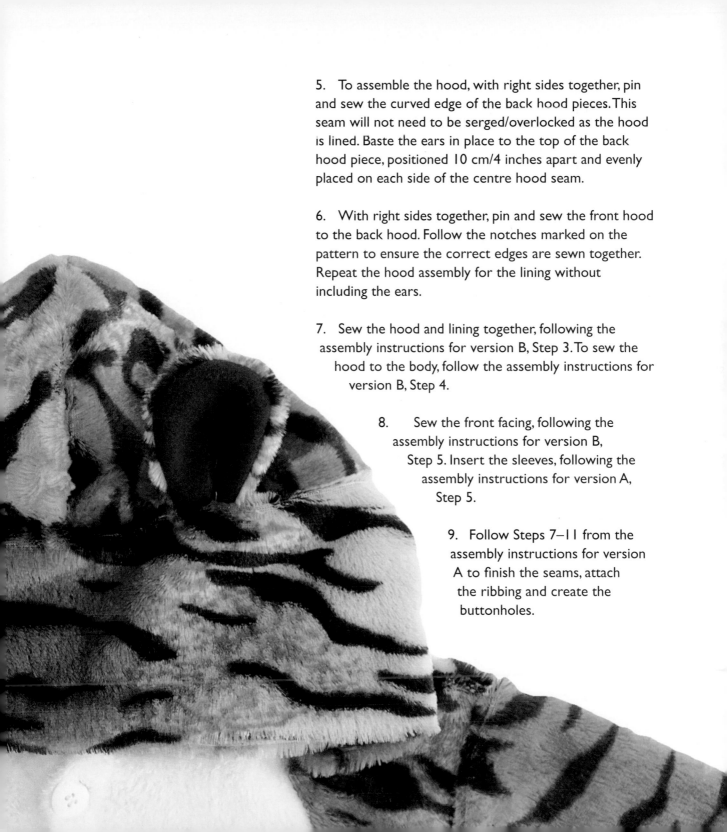

5. To assemble the hood, with right sides together, pin and sew the curved edge of the back hood pieces. This seam will not need to be serged/overlocked as the hood is lined. Baste the ears in place to the top of the back hood piece, positioned 10 cm/4 inches apart and evenly placed on each side of the centre hood seam.

6. With right sides together, pin and sew the front hood to the back hood. Follow the notches marked on the pattern to ensure the correct edges are sewn together. Repeat the hood assembly for the lining without including the ears.

7. Sew the hood and lining together, following the assembly instructions for version B, Step 3. To sew the hood to the body, follow the assembly instructions for version B, Step 4.

8. Sew the front facing, following the assembly instructions for version B, Step 5. Insert the sleeves, following the assembly instructions for version A, Step 5.

9. Follow Steps 7–11 from the assembly instructions for version A to finish the seams, attach the ribbing and create the buttonholes.

Reindeer

Not only will this snug Reindeer onesie keep out the winter chill it also makes the perfect outfit for late night Santa watching on Christmas Eve. Be careful not to be spotted with that big red nose.

Cutting

The fabric requirements for this onesie are listed in the measurement chart on pages 8–9. Use the pattern pieces from version B, together with these additional pieces from the Reindeer template page:

Ears:	Cut 1 pair from the main fabric and one pair from contrast fabric.
Antler:	Cut 2 pairs from the main fabric.
Outer eye:	Cut 1 pair from white felt.
Inner eye:	Cut 1 pair from grey felt.
Pupil:	Cut 1 pair from black felt.
Nose:	Cut a 15 cm/6 inches diameter circle from red fabric or buy a red nose.
Tail:	Cut 1 from main fabric and one in contrast fabric.

Cut the front insert from contrast fabric. Cut the hood lining pieces from a second contrast fabric, in the same colour as the outer hood but of a lighter weight, to avoid too much bulk at the neckline seam.

Assembly

All the seam allowances are 1.5 cm/⁵/₈ inch.

1. With right sides together, pin the tail pieces. Sew around the curved edges and leave the straight side open. Trim the seam allowance to 6 mm/¹/₄ inch on the curved end. Turn the tail through to the right side, and baste a double fold into the base.

2. Baste the tail to the right side of the centre back seam, positioning it 18 cm/7 inches up from the crotch.

3. For the centre back seam follow the assembly instructions for version A, Step 1. For the front insert follow the assembly instructions for version B, Step 1. For the shoulder seams follow the assembly instructions for version A, Step 2.

4. Place one ear from the main fabric and one from the contrast fabric with right sides together. Pin, and sew around the curved edge, leaving the straight edge open. Trim the seam to 6 mm/¹/₄ inch. Turn the ears to the right side and baste a 2 cm/³/₄ inch-wide pleat into the base of each ear.

5. For the antlers, if you want them to be stiff then apply interfacing to the pieces before sewing. With right sides together, pin and sew around the antler shape. Use the sewing template provided to determine the correct stitch line. Leave the straight end open. Trim the seam allowance to 6 mm/¹/₄ inch, clip into the corners, and turn right side out.

6. To assemble the hood, with right sides together, pin and sew the curved edge of the back hood pieces. This seam will not need to be serged/overlocked as the hood is lined. Baste the ears and antlers in place on the top of the back hood piece. Position the antlers 5 cm/2 inches apart and the ears 20 cm/8 inches apart, on each side of the centre hood seam.

7. With right sides together pin and sew the front hood to the back hood. Follow the notches marked on the pattern to ensure the correct edges are sewn together. Repeat the hood assembly process for the lining, without including the ears and antlers.

8. To create the face, attach the pre-cut template pieces to the front hood using a zig zag stitch set on a short stitch length. Attach the pieces, excluding the nose, in the following order:
- Stitch the pupil onto the inner eye.
- Stitch the inner eye to the outer eye.
- Stitch the eyes onto the front hood, placing them equal distances from the centre.

9. Sew the hood and lining together, following the assembly instructions for version B, Step 3. Sew the hood to the body following the assembly instructions for Version B, Step 4.

10. Sew the front facing following the assembly instructions for Version B, Step 5. Attach the sleeves following the assembly instructions for Version A, Step 5.

11. Follow Steps 7–11 from the assembly instructions for Version A to finish the seams, attach the ribbing and create the buttonholes.

12. Finally, attach the nose. If you are creating the nose from the template then sew a gathering stitch around the outer edge of the circle. Pull the gathers up until the desired size is achieved, then stuff with fibrefill. Hand sew the nose to the centre front of the hood.

Elf

Wrap your child up in this warm and super-cute Elf onesie. If you have a whole tribe they would also make perfect Christmas gifts for Santa's little helpers.

Cutting

The fabric requirements are listed in the measurement chart on pages 8–9. Follow the assembly instructions and pattern pieces for Version A, together with these pieces from the Elf template page:

Hood trim: Cut one piece from red felt (after the hood is sewn).

Neck trim: Cut from red felt. The amount required depends on the neckline size.

You will also need an additional 50 cm/20 inches of contrast fabric for the sleeves. Cut all pieces from the main fabric, except the sleeves, which should be cut in contrast. Cut two pairs of the hood for this style, as it will be lined. The hood can be lined in the same colour fabric as the outer hood, however choose a lighter weight fabric for the lining to avoid bulk at the neck seam.

Assembly

All the seam allowances are 1.5 cm/⅝ inch.

1. Follow Steps 1, 2 and 3 from the assembly instructions for Version A.

2. Before attaching the red felt to the hood, cut the felt to match the length of the front hood section. Then topsitich the felt in place to the right side of the hood.

3. To sew the hood to the lining, with right sides together pin the long edge of the front hood main fabric to the front hood lining fabric. Sew, using a 2.5 cm/ 1 inch seam allowance, then trim it back to 1.5 cm/⅝ inch. Turn the hood to the right side, and topstitch along this edge to stop the lining from rolling

out of place. Baste the hood and lining together around the neckline edge. This will make sewing the hood to the body easier.

4.   Using the neck trim template, cut out as many triangles as you need to edge the opening. Place the triangles around the neckline, point downward, and overlapping as you go. Leave a 2.5 cm/1 inch gap at the front opening to allow for the front facing to be turned back later.

5.   Baste the triangles in place. As you sew, place a small tuck in the triangles that fall over the shoulder seam. This will aid the straight edge of the triangle in curving around the neck shape.

6.   Sew the hood to the body, following the assembly instructions for Version B, Step 4. Sew the front facing following the assembly instructions for Version B, Step 5. Insert the sleeves, following the assembly instructions for Version A, Step 5.

7.   Follow Steps 7–11 from the assembly instructions for Version A to finish the seams, attach the ribbing and create the buttonholes.

Cow

No book on onesies would be complete without a classic Cow design. The kids will just love to bring the farmyard inside wearing this soft and funky outfit.

Cutting

The fabric requirements are listed in the measurement chart on pages 8–9. Use the assembly instructions and pattern pieces from Version A for the body, and from Version B for the hood, together with these additional pieces from the Cow template page:

Ears: Cut 1 pair from main fabric and one pair from a contrast fabric.

Tail: Cut 1 piece 50 x 10 cm/20 x 4 inches from the main fabric.

Cut out all the body pieces in cow-printed fabric, and cut the hood lining pieces and inside ears in contrast fabric. If possible, choose a lighter weight fabric to avoid bulk at the neck seam. You will also need a small piece of black fur, or similar, for the tail end.

Assembly

All the seam allowances are 1.5 cm/⁵⁄₈ inch.

1. Baste the black fur onto the end of the tail and fold the tail in half lengthwise. With right sides together sew the long raw edges together, leaving one end open. Trim the corners and turn the tail through to the right side.

```
fold
```

2. Position the tail on the right side of the centre back seam, 23 cm/9 inches up from the crotch, and baste in place.

3. For the centre back seam, follow the assembly instructions for Version A, Step 1, and for the shoulder seams follow Version A, Step 2.

4. For the ears, place one ear piece from the main fabric and one from the contrast fabric with right sides together. Pin and sew around the curved edge, leaving the straight edge open. Trim the seam to 6 mm/¹⁄₄ inch and turn to the right side. Baste a 1.5 cm/⁵⁄₈ inch-wide pleat into the base of the ear.

5. With right sides together, pin and sew the curved edge of the back hood pieces together. This seam will not need to be serged/overlocked as the hood is lined.

Creating a face

As the main fabric is patterned I have not created a face. However, if you wish to add eyes or a nose then refer to 'Create the Face' section from another similar design.

6.   Position the ears on the top of the hood back piece, 12.5 cm/5 inches apart of the centre hood seam, placed evenly on each side. Baste in place. With right sides together, pin and sew the front hood to the back hood. Follow the notches marked on the pattern to ensure the correct edges are sewn together. Repeat the hood assembly for the lining without including the ears.

7.   Sew the hood and the lining together following the assembly instructions for Version B, Step 3, then sew the hood to the body following the assembly instructions for Version B, Step 4.

8.   Sew the front facing following the assembly instructions for Version B, Step 5, then insert the sleeves following the assembly instructions for Version A, Step 5.

9.   Follow Steps 7–11 from the assembly instructions for Version A to finish the seams, attach the ribbing and create the buttonholes.

Duck

This little Duck onesie is so bright and happy that sewing it just made my day. I think this design may be my favourite, and I just couldn't help dressing my daughter in this one for the photo shoot.

Cutting

The fabric requirements are listed in the measurement chart on pages 8–9. Use the pattern pieces for Version B plus additional pieces from the Duck template page:

Head comb: Cut 1 pair from main fabric and from fabric stabiliser.

Outer eye: Cut 1 pair from white felt.

Inner eye: Cut 1 pair from black felt.

Pupil: Cut 1 pair from white felt.

Beak: Cut 1 pair from orange felt and cut 1 from lightweight batting (wadding).

Tail: Cut 1 pair from main fabric and from fabric stabiliser.

Cut the front insert and inside hood pieces from contrast fabric.

Assembly

All the seam allowances are 1.5 cm/⁵⁄₈ inch.

1. Apply stabilising fabric to the tail pieces. With right sides together, pin and sew the curved edges of the tail, leaving the straight end open. Trim the seam allowance on the curved edges back to 6 mm/¹⁄₄ inch and turn through to the right side.

2. Position the tail on the right side of the centre back seam, 20 cm/8 inches up from the crotch, and baste in place.

3. For the centre back seam follow the assembly instructions for Version A, Step 1, and for the front insert follow the assembly instructions for Version B, Step 1. For the shoulder seams follow the assembly instructions for Version A, Step 2.

4. For the head comb, apply stabilising fabric to the pieces, then with right sides together, pin and sew around the head comb shape. Use the sewing template provided to determine the correct stitch line, and leave the straight end open. Trim the seam allowance to 6 mm/¹⁄₄ inch, clip into the corners and turn right side out.

5. To assemble the hood, with right sides together, pin and sew the curved edge of the back hood pieces. This seam will not need to be serged/overlocked as the hood

It is best to avoid using an iron on the right side of synthetic fleece and fur fabric. Therefore it is suggested to choose stable fabrics such as felt for the facial features, and pin them into place before sewing, rather than using a fusible web that requires ironing. For additional stability place a piece of tear-away stabiliser behind the area that is being sewn.

is lined. Baste the head comb to the centre of the back hood piece. With right sides together, pin and sew the front hood to the back hood, following the notches marked on the pattern to ensure the correct edges are sewn together. Repeat the hood assembly for the lining, but without the head comb piece.

6. To create the face, attach the pre-cut template pieces to the front hood using a zig zag stitch set on a short stitch length. Attach in the following order:
*   Stitch the pupil onto the inner eye.
*   Stitch the inner eye onto the outer eye.
*   Stitch the eyes onto the front hood, evenly positioned each side of the centre.

7. To create the beak, with right sides together, pin the batting and beak pieces together and sew around the curved edge. Leave the straight edge open. Trim the curved seam to 6 mm/^{1}/$_4$ inch, turn to the right side, and baste the beak to the centre of the front hood.

8. Sew the hood and lining together following the assembly instructions for Version B, Step 3, then sew the hood to the body following the assembly instructions for Version B, Step 4.

9. Sew the front facing following the assembly instructions for Version B, Step 5. Insert the sleeves following the instructions for Version A, Step 5.

10. Follow Steps 7–11 from the assembly instructions for Version A to finish the seams, attach the ribbing and create the buttonholes.

Pig

Certainly a favourite design with my kids, this Pig onesie is outrageously cute. The curly tail, folded ears and piggy nose may need a little more effort than some of the simpler designs, but the end result is definitely worth it.

Cutting

The fabric requirements are listed in the measurement chart on page 8–9. Use the pattern pieces from Version B, together with additional pieces from the Pig template page:

Ears: Cut 2 pairs from main fabric.

Eyes: Cut 1 pair from white felt.

Pupil: Cut 1 pair from black felt.

Nose: Cut 2 from the main fabric (plus stabiliser fabric).

Nose side: Cut 1 from the main fabric (plus stabiliser fabric).

Tail: Cut 1 piece from main fabric 25 x 9 cm (10 x 3½ inches).

Cut the front insert in contrast fabric. Cut the hood lining pieces from a second contrast fabric, which is the same colour as the outer hood, but a lighter weight of fabric to avoid too much bulk at the neckline seam.

You will also need 17 cm/7 inches of 6 mm/¼ inch-wide elastic, two black 1 cm/³/₈ inch buttons, and a small amount of fibrefill to stuff the nose.

Assembly

All the seam allowances are 1.5 cm/⅝ inch.

1. To make the tail, with right sides together, fold the tail piece in half lengthwise and sew the raw edges together, leaving one end open. To achieve a curved end to the tail, finish one end with a curved stitch line. Sew the piece of elastic on top of the existing straight stitch line, stretching it while sewing to fit the total length of the tail. This will encourage the tail to curl. Trim the seam allowance on the curved end to 6 mm/¼ inch, and turn right side out.

fold

2. Position the tail on the right side of the centre back seam, 23 cm/9 inches up from the crotch, and baste in place.

3. For the centre back seam, follow the assembly instructions for Version A, Step 1. For the front insert, follow the assembly instructions for Version B, Step 1. For the shoulder seams, follow the assembly instructions for Version A, Step 2.

4. To make the ears, with right sides together pin and sew around the curved edge of the ears, leaving the straight edge open. Trim the seam to 6 mm/¼ inch, then turn right side out. Sew across the stitching/fold line as marked on the template.

5. To assemble the hood, with right sides together, pin and sew the curved edge of the back hood pieces, this seam will not need to be serged/overlocked as the hood is lined. Baste the ears in place to the top of the hood back piece, 10 cm/ 4 inches apart, and evenly placed either side of the centre hood seam. With right sides together, pin and sew the front hood to the back hood. Follow the notches marked on the pattern to ensure the correct edges are sewn together.

It is best to avoid using an iron on the right side of synthetic fleece and fur fabric. Therefore it is suggested to choose stable fabrics such as felt for the facial features, and pin them into place before sewing, rather than using a fusible web that requires ironing. For additional stability place a piece of tear-away stabiliser behind the area that is being sewn.

Repeat the hood assembly for the lining without including the ears.

6.   To create the face, attach the pre-cut template pieces to the front hood using a zig zag stitch set on a short stitch length. First stitch the pupil onto the eye, then stitch the eyes onto the front hood, evenly positioned apart from the centre.

7.   To sew the hood and lining together follow the assembly instructions for Version B, Step 3, then sew the hood to the body following the assembly instructions for Version B, Step 4.

8.   Sew the front facing following the assembly instructions for Version B, Step 5, then insert the sleeves following the assembly instructions for Version A, Step 5.

9.   Follow Steps 7–11 from the assembly instructions for Version A to finish the seams, attach the ribbing and create the buttonholes.

10. Now create the nose. Apply stabilising fabric to the nose pieces, and with right sides together sew the two short ends of the nose side piece together. With right sides together sew one of the circular nose pieces to the nose side piece. Turn right side out.

Hand sew the two black buttons onto the nose front. With right sides together sew the remaining nose piece to the nose sides. Leave an opening in this seam and then turn through. Stuff the nose lightly with fibrefill, then hand sew the opening closed. Position the nose on the face and hand sew into place.

11. Fold the ears forward along the previously made stitch line and hand sew a few stitches through all layers to keep in place.

Monkey

I don't think one monkey is enough. This adorable little fellow would look best with at least two other friends. Better get the bananas; it's time to monkey around.

Cutting

The fabric requirements are listed in the measurement chart on pages 8–9. Refer to the pattern pieces for Version B, together with additional pieces from the Monkey template page:

Outer Ears: Cut 2 pairs from the main fabric
Inner Ears: Cut 1 pair from contrast fabric
Eye: Cut 1 pair from white felt
Pupil: Cut 1 pair from black felt
Face: Cut 1 from white or brown felt
Tail: Cut 1 piece 50 x 10 cm/20 x 4 inches from main fabric

Cut the front insert from contrast fabric. Cut the hood lining pieces from second contrast fabric, which should be the same colour as the outer hood, but in a lighter weight fabric to avoid too much bulk at the neckline seam.

You will also need a 38 cm/15 in piece of 6 mm/¼ inch-wide elastic.

Assembly

All the seam allowances are 1.5 cm/⁵/₈ inch.

1.   With right sides together, fold the tail in half lengthwise and sew the raw edges together, leaving one end open. To achieve a curved end to the tail, finish one end with a curved stitch line. Sew the length of elastic on top of the existing straight stitch line, stretching it while sewing so that it fits the total length of the tail. This will encourage it to curl. Trim the seam allowance on the curved end to 6 mm/¹/₄ inch, and turn right side out.

fold

2.   Position the tail on the centre back seam, 20 cm/ 8 inches up from the crotch, and baste in place.

3.   For the centre back seam, follow the assembly instructions for Version A, Step 1. For the front insert follow the assembly instructions for Version B, Step 1. For the shoulder seams follow the instructions for Version A, Step 2.

4.   For the ears, position the wrong side of the inner ear onto the right side of the outer ear. The inner ear should meet on the straight edge, but sit 2.5 cm/1 inch in from the outer ear curved edge. Stitch the inner ear in place with a zig zag stitch. With right sides together, pin and sew the front and back ears together around the curved edge, leaving the straight edge open. Trim the seam to 6 mm/¹/₄ inch and turn right side out.

5.   To assemble the hood, with right sides together, pin and sew the long curved edge of the back hood pieces. This seam will not need to be serged/overlocked as the hood is lined. Position the ears on the top of the hood back piece, 15 cm/6 inches apart, and evenly placed on each side of the centre hood seam. Baste in place. With right sides together, pin and sew the front hood to the back hood. Follow the notches marked on the pattern to ensure the correct edges are sewn together. Repeat the hood assembly instructions for the lining without including the ears.

6.   To create the face, attach the pre-cut template pieces to the front hood using a zig zag stitch set on a short stitch length. Attach in the following order:
- Stitch the pupil onto the eye.
- Stitch the eyes onto the curved face.
- Stitch the curved face onto the centre of the front hood, the lower edge should match up with the hood edge so that it will be sewn into the hood lining seam.

7.   Sew the hood and lining together following the assembly instructions for Version B, Step 3. Sew the hood to the body following the assembly instructions for Version B, Step 4.

8.   Sew the front facing following the assembly instructions for Version B, Step 5. Then insert the sleeves following the assembly instructions for Version A, Step 5.

9.   Follow Steps 7–11 from the assembly instructions for Version A to finish the seams, attach the ribbing and create the buttonholes.

Bunny

Perfect for an Easter egg hunt, this delightful Bunny onesie will have the kids hopping with happiness. Don't be afraid to swap the colours around here. Pink or pale blue bunnies are just as cute.

Cutting

The fabric requirements are listed in the measurement chart on pages 8–9. Refer to the pattern pieces from Version B, together with additional pieces from the Bunny template page:

Ears: Cut 1 pair from the main fabric and 1 pair from contast fabric.
Eyes: Cut 1 pair from black felt.
Pupil: Cut one pair from white felt.
Teeth: Cut 1 from white felt.
Tail: Cut 1 from main fabric.

Cut the front insert from contrast fabric. Cut the hood lining pieces from second contrast fabric, which should be in the same colour as the outer hood, but choose a lighter weight fabric to avoid too much bulk at the neckline seam.

You will also need a small amount of fibrefill to stuff the tail.

Assembly

All the seam allowances are 1.5 cm/⅝ inch.

1.   First create the tail. Sew a gathering stitch around the outer edge of the tail piece by using the longest stitch length on your sewing machine. Do not back stitch at the beginning or the end. Pull up on the bobbin threads until the tail begins to gather and form a ball. Once the desired tail shape is achieved, lightly stuff the tail with fibrefill and knot the thread ends.

2.   Position the tail on the right side of the centre back seam, 23 cm/9 inches up from the crotch. Baste the tail into place, flattening it as you do so. Alternatively, hand-sew the tail onto the back after the seam has been created.

3.   For the centre back seam, follow the assembly instructions for Version A, Step 1. For the front insert, follow the assembly instructions for Version B, Step 1. For the shoulder seams, follow the assembly instructions for Version A, Step 2.

4.   Place one ear piece from the main fabric and one from the contrast fabric with right sides together. Pin and sew around the curved edge, leaving the straight edge open. Trim the seam to 6 mm/¼ inch and turn to the correct side. Baste a 2.5 cm/1 inch-wide pleat into the base of the ear.

Using an iron

It is best to avoid using an iron on the right side of synthetic fleece and fur fabric. Therefore it is suggested to choose stable fabrics such as felt for the facial features, and pin them into place before sewing, rather than using a fusible web that requires ironing. For additional stability place a piece of tear-away stabiliser behind the area that is being sewn.

5. Next assemble the hood. With right sides together, pin and sew the curved edge of the back hood pieces. This seam will not need to be serged/overlocked as the hood is lined. Position the ears on the top of the hood back piece, 12.5 cm/5 inches apart, and evenly placed at each side of the centre hood seam. Baste in place. With right sides together, pin and sew the front hood to the back hood. Follow the notches marked on the pattern to ensure the correct edges are sewn together. Repeat the hood assembly steps for the lining without including the ears.

6. To create the face, attach the pre-cut template pieces to the front hood using a zig zag stitch set on a short stitch length. Attach in the following order:
- Stitch the pupil onto the eye.
- Stitch the eyes onto the front hood, evenly positioned apart from the centre.
- Baste the teeth to the centre of the front hood.

7. Sew the hood and lining together following the assembly instructions for Version B, Step 3. Sew the hood to the body following the assembly instructions for Version B, Step 4.

8. Sew the front facing following the assembly instructions for Version B, Step 5. Insert the sleeves following the assembly instructions for Version A, Step 5.

9. Follow Steps 7–11 from the assembly instructions for Version A to finish the seams, attach the ribbing and create the buttonholes.

Dinosaur

Don't be fooled by this scary green dinosaur; he may look nasty but underneath he is just a big softy. All those spikes take a bit of time to prepare, but it wouldn't be a proper dinosaur without them.

Cutting

The fabric requirements are listed in the measurement chart on pages 8–9. Use the pattern pieces for Version B, together with additional pieces from the Dinosaur template page:

Head spikes: Cut 5 pairs from contrast fabric and from stabilising fabric.

Eye: Cut 1 pair from white felt.

Pupil: Cut 1 pair from black felt.

Jaw: Cut 1 from the main fabric and cut 1 from second contrast fabric.

Teeth: Cut 5 from white felt.

Tail: Cut 1 pair from the main fabric and from light weight batting (wadding).

Tail Spikes: Cut 3 pairs from contrast fabric.

Cut the front insert from contrast fabric and the hood lining pieces from second contrast fabric, (red).

Assembly

All the seam allowances are 1.5 cm/⁵/₈ inch.

1.   To make the tail spikes, with right sides together, pin and sew around the curved edges of the spikes, leaving the straight edge open. Trim the seam allowance on the curved edges to 6 mm/¹/₄ inch and turn right side out.

2.   Position the spikes along the top edge of one of the tail pieces, raw edges aligned. The first spike should be 6 cm/ 2¹/₂ inches from the straight edge of the tail, leave a 1.2 cm/ ¹/₂ inch gap between the remaining spikes. Baste in place.

3.   Apply the batting to the wrong side of the tail piece. With right sides together, pin and sew through all thicknesses around the curved edges of the tail, leaving the straight end open. Trim the seam allowance on the curved edges to 6 mm/¹/₄ inch and turn through to the right side. Position the tail on the right side of the centre back seam, 15 cm/6 inches up from the crotch, and baste in place.

4.   For the centre back seam, follow the assembly instructions for Version A, Step 1. For the front insert, follow the assembly instructions for Version B, Step 1. For the shoulder seams, follow the assembly instructions for Version A, Step 2.

5.   To make the head spikes, apply the stabilising fabric to the head spike pieces. With right sides together, pin and sew around the curved edges, leaving the straight ends open. Trim the seam allowances to 6 mm/¹/₄ inch and turn to the right side.

6.   Baste the head spikes onto the curved edge of one of the back hood pieces. Position the first head spike 2.5 cm/1 inch back from the straight edge and then leave a 1.2 cm/¹/₂ inch gap between each remaining spike.

7.   To assemble the hood, with right sides together, pin and sew the curved edge of the back hood pieces. This seam will not need to be serged/overlocked as the hood is lined. With right sides together, pin and sew the front hood to the back hood. Follow the notches marked on the pattern to ensure the correct edges are sewn together. Repeat the hood assembly for the lining without including the head spikes.

8.   To create the face, attach the pre-cut template pieces to the front hood using a zig zag stitch set on a short stitch length. Attach in the following order:
- Stitch the pupil onto the eye.
- Stitch the eyes onto the front hood, evenly positioned apart from the centre.

9.   To create the jaw., position the straight edge of the teeth around the curved edge of the jaw, leaving a 2 cm/3/4 inch gap at each end to allow for the seam. Baste in place. With right sides together, pin and sew around the curved edges of the two jaw pieces, leaving the straight edge open. Trim the curved seam to 6 mm/1/4 inch and turn to the right side. Topstitch around the curved edge to keep the lining from rolling out. Baste the jaw to the centre of the front hood.

10.   Sew the hood and lining together following the assembly instructions for Version B, Step 3.
   Sew the hood to the body following the assembly instructions for Version B, Step 4. Sew the front facing following the assembly instructions for Version B, Step 5. Insert the sleeves following the assembly instructions for Version A, Step 5.

11.   Follow Steps 7–11 from the assembly instructions for Version A to finish the seams, attach the ribbing and create the buttonholes.

Leopard

This Leopard onesie began its life as a throw rug, and I just knew it would look so much better as a leopard. Don't be held back by fabric choices, onesies will work in just about any material.

Cutting

The fabric requirements are listed in the measurement chart on pages 8–9. Use the pattern pieces for Version B, together with additional pieces from the Leopard template page:

Ears: Cut 2 pairs from the main fabric
Tail: Cut 1 piece 50 x 10 cm/20 x 4 inches from the main fabric

Cut the front insert from contrast fabric (white) and cut the hood lining pieces from a second contrast fabric (brown).

Assembly

All seams are 1.5 cm/⅝ inch.

1. With right sides together, fold the tail in half lengthwise and sew the raw edges together, leaving one end open. To achieve a curved end to the tail, finish one end with a curved stitch line. Trim the seam allowance on the curved end to 6 mm/¼ inch, and turn through to the right side.

fold

2. Position the tail on the centre back seam, 23 cm/ 9 inches up from the crotch and baste in place.

3. For the centre back seam, follow the assembly instructions for Version A, Step 1. For the front insert, follow the assembly instructions for Version B, Step 1. For the shoulder seams, follow the assembly instructions for Version A, Step 2.

4. To assemble the ears, with right sides together pin and sew around the curved edges, leaving the straight edges open. Trim the seam to 6 mm/¼ inch and turn to the right side.

5. Now assemble the hood. With right sides together, pin and sew the curved edge of the back hood pieces. This seam will not need to be serged/overlocked as the hood is lined. Position the ears on the top of the hood back piece, 6 cm/2½ inches apart and evenly placed on each side of the centre hood seam. Baste in place.

Creating a face

As the main fabric is patterned I have not created a face. However, if you wish to add eyes or a nose then refer to 'Create the Face' section from another similar design.

6. With right sides together, pin and sew the front hood to the back hood. Follow the notches marked on the pattern to ensure the correct edges are sewn together. Repeat the hood assembly for the lining; without including the ears.

7. Sew the hood and lining together following the assembly instructions for Version B, Step 3.
   Sew the hood to the body following the assembly instructions for Version B, Step 4.

8. Sew the front facing following the assembly instructions for Version B, Step 5, and insert the sleeves following the assembly instructions for Version A, Step 5.

9. Follow Steps 7–11 from the assembly instructions for Version A to finish the seams, attach the ribbing and create the buttonholes.

Pirate

Ahoy matey! This pirate shows that onesies don't always need to be animals. Get creative and use any combination of fabrics to create this jolly lad.

Cutting

The fabric requirements are listed in the measurement chart on pages 8–9. Use the pattern pieces from Version A for the body and the pattern pieces from Version B for the hood, with these additional pieces from the Pirate template page or pattern sheet:

Eye patch: Cut 1 from black felt, leather or vinyl, (or purchase a pre-made patch).

Vest: Cut 1 pair from red stripe and one pair in white poplin.

You will also need:
50 cm/20 inches white fabric, for the sleeves.
50 cm/20 inches red stripe fabric, for the vest.
50 cm/20 inches poplin fabric, for the vest.
1 red bandana.

Cut the front, back, back hood and hood lining pieces from the main fabric. Cut the sleeves from white, and cut the front hood from a red bandana.

Assembly

All the seam allowances are 1.5 cm/⁵⁄₈ inch.

1. For the centre back seam, follow the assembly instructions for Version A, Step 1.

2. Create the vest. With right sides together, pin and sew the vest main pieces to the vest lining pieces. Sew around the armhole, lower edge and front neckline. Trim these seams to 6 mm/¹⁄₄ inch. Leave the shoulder seam, side seam and centre front seams open and turn the vest to the right side. Baste the vest onto the front at the shoulder, side and centre front.

Fabric choices

If you choose a woven poplin fabric for lining the vest it will help to keep the finished edges in shape after the vest is turned through.

3. For the shoulder seams follow the assembly instructions for Version A, Step 2.

4. To assemble the hood, with right sides together, pin and sew the curved edge of the back hood pieces. This seam will not need to be serged/overlocked as the hood is lined. With right sides together, pin and sew the front hood to the back hood. Follow the notches marked on the pattern to ensure the correct edges are sewn together. Repeat the hood assembly for the lining.

5. Position the eye patch 2.5 cm/1 inch to the right of the centre on the front hood piece, and baste in place.

6. Sew the hood and lining together following the assembly instructions for Version B, Step 3. Sew the hood to the body following the assembly instructions for Version B, Step 4.

7. Sew the front facing following the assembly instructions for Version B, Step 5. Insert the sleeves following the assembly instructions for Version A, Step 5.

8. Follow Steps 7–11 from the assembly instructions for Version A to finish the seams, attach the ribbing and create the buttonholes.

Lady Beetle

Little Lady Beetle is so delightful, and such fun to make. I couldn't believe my luck when I realised that the front insert shape was also the perfect shape for the wings!

Cutting

The fabric requirements are listed in the measurement chart on pages 8–9. Use the pattern pieces for Version B together with additional pieces from the Lady Beetle template page:

Antennae: Cut 2 pairs from contrast fabric.
Eye: Cut 1 pair from white felt.
Pupil: Cut 1 pair in black felt.
Wings: Use the front insert pattern piece from Version B to create the wings; cut 1 pair from the main fabric, 1 pair from black lining fabric and 1 pair from stabilising fabric.

Cut the body and sleeves from the main fabric. Cut the front insert and hood pieces from contrast fabric. Cut the hood lining pieces from a second contrast fabric; this should be the same colour as the outer hood, but in a lighter weight fabric to avoid too much bulk at the neckline seam.

Assembly

All the seam allowances are 1.5 cm/⁵/₈ inch.

1.   For the centre back seam, follow the assembly instructions for Version A, Step 1.

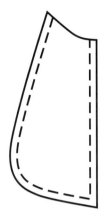

2.   To create the wings, apply the stabilising fabric to the lining pieces. With right sides together, place one main piece and one lining piece together. Sew around the long straight edge and the long curved edge, leaving the top neck edge open. Trim this seam to 6 mm/¹/₄ inch, and turn right side out. Baste the wings to the back neck edge.

3.   For the front insert, follow the assembly instructions for Version B, Step 1. For the shoulder seams, follow the assembly instructions for Version A, Step 2.

4.   For the antennae, with right sides together, pin and sew around the curved edges, leaving the straight edges open. Trim the seam to 6 mm/¹/₄ inch and turn right ` side out.

5.   To assemble the hood, with right sides together, pin and sew the curved edge of the back hood pieces. This seam will not need to be serged/overlocked as the hood is lined. Position the antennae on the top of the hood back piece 10 cm/4 inches apart and evenly placed at each side of the centre hood seam. Baste in place.

6.   With right sides together, pin and sew the front hood to the back hood. Follow the notches marked on the pattern to ensure the correct edges are sewn together. Repeat the hood assembly for the lining without including the antennae.

Attaching the wings

If your main fabric is thick then adding the wings into the neck seam will create too much bulk. The alternative is to serge/overlock the top edge of the wings and topstitch the wings into place just below the stitching line on the back neck. Therefore the wings will not be enclosed into the back neck seam.

7. Now create the face. Attach the pre-cut template pieces to the front hood using a zig zag stitch set on a short stitch length. Attach in the following order:
- Stitch the pupil onto the eye.
- Stitch the eyes onto the front hood, evenly positioned apart from the centre.

8. Sew the hood and lining together following the assembly instructions for Version B, Step 3. Sew the hood to the body following the assembly instructions for Version B, Step 4.

9. Sew the front facing following the assembly instructions for Version B, Step 5. Insert the sleeves., by following the assembly instructions for Version A, Step 5.

10. Follow Steps 7–11 from the assembly instructions for Version A to finish the seams, attach the ribbing and create the buttonholes.

Zebra

Super soft and comfortable, your child will want to stay on the wild side all day long in this great Zebra onesie. Don't be limited by local fabric stores, many of the Onesie fabrics in the book, including this one, were sourced on-line.

Cutting

The fabric requirements are listed in the measurement chart on pages 8–9. Use the pattern pieces for Version B, together with additional pieces from the Zebra template page:

Ears: Cut 1 pair from the main fabric, and one pair in black or white contrast

Tail: Cut 1 from the main fabric

Cut the front insert from contrast fabric (white). Cut the hood lining pieces from a second contrast fabric. This can be either black or white but try to use a lighter weight fabric than the front insert to avoid too much bulk at the neck seam.

You will also need a 76 cm/30 inches suede fringe as an additional trim. This can be found in party shops, or online. Alternatively, use the same length of 5 cm/2 inches wide black felt, and cut fine strips cut into it with scissors.

87

Assembly

All the seam allowances are 1.5 cm/⅝ inch.

1. With right sides together, fold the tail piece in half lengthwise and sew the raw edges together. Leave the wider end open and turn through to right side. Fold up a 15 cm/6 inch piece of the fringe and topstitch to the tail end.

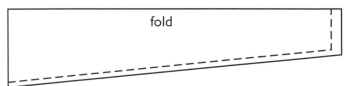

2. Position the tail on the centre back seam 23 cm/ 9 inches up from the crotch and baste in place. For the centre back seam follow the assembly instructions for Version A, Step 1.

3. For the front insert follow the assembly instructions for Version B, Step 1, and for the shoulder seams follow the assembly instructions for Version A, Step 2.

4. To assemble the ears, with right sides together, pin and sew around the curved edges, leaving the straight edge open. Trim the seam to 6 mm/¼ inch and turn the ears to the correct side. Fold the outer sides of the ears towards the front to meet in the centre and create a pleat.

Creating a face

As the main fabric is patterned I have not created a face. However, if you wish to add eyes or a nose then refer to 'Create the Face' section from another similar design.

5. For the hood, baste the fringe onto one of the back hood pieces, positioned on the long curved edge. With right sides together, pin and sew the curved edge of the back hood pieces. This seam will not need to be serged/overlocked as the hood is lined.

6. Position the ears on the top of the hood back piece, 9 cm/3½ inches apart and evenly placed on each side of the centre hood seam. Baste in place. With right sides together, pin and sew the front hood to the back hood. Follow the notches marked on the pattern to ensure the correct edges are sewn together. Repeat the hood assembly for the lining without including the ears or fringe.

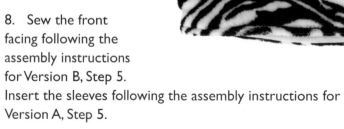

7. Sew the hood and lining together following the assembly instructions for Version B, Step 3. Sew the hood to the body following the assembly instructions for Version B, Step 4.

8. Sew the front facing following the assembly instructions for Version B, Step 5. Insert the sleeves following the assembly instructions for Version A, Step 5.

9. Follow Steps 7–11 from the assembly instructions for Version A to finish the seams, attach the ribbing and create the buttonholes.

Elephant

I love this Elephant design, it has so much character! With those floppy ears and a long trunk, this onesie is loads of fun. If you want to make two, aqua looks great as well as grey.

Cutting

The fabric requirements are listed in the measurement chart on pages 8–9. Use the pattern pieces for Version B, together with additional pieces from the Elephant template page:

Ears: Cut 1 pair from the main fabric and one pair in contrast fabric

Eye: Cut 1 pair from white felt

Pupil: Cut 1 pair from black felt

Trunk: Cut 1 pair from the main fabric

Tail: Cut 1 from the main fabric

Cut the front insert from contrast fabric. Cut the hood lining pieces from the second contrast fabric, this should be the same colour as the outer hood, but choose a lighter weight fabric to avoid too much bulk at the neckline seam.

You will also need:

- 7.5 x 15 cm/3 x 6 inch piece of felt for the tail end, the same colour as the main fabric
- A small amount of fibrefill to stuff the nose

Assembly

All the seam allowances are 1.5 cm/⁵/₈ inch.

1. Create five folds in the tail end felt piece and baste to the tail end. With right sides together, fold the tail in half lengthwise and sew the raw edges together, leaving the wider end open. Turn the tail through to right side. Cut strips into the felt to create a fringe.

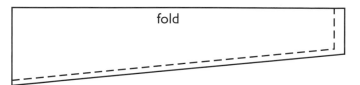

fold

2. Position the tail on the centre back seam, 23 cm/ 9 inches up from the crotch, and baste in place.

3. For the centre back seam, follow the assembly instructions for Version A, Step 1. For the front insert, follow the assembly instructions for Version B, Step 1. For the shoulder seams, follow the assembly instructions for Version A, Step 2.

4. Next, assemble the ears. With right sides together, pin an ear piece in the main fabric to an ear piece from contrast fabric and sew around the curved edges. Leave the straight edges open. Trim the seam to 6 mm/¹/₄ inch and turn right side out.

5. Now assemble the hood. With right sides together, pin and sew the curved edge of the back hood pieces. This seam will not need to be serged/overlocked as the hood is lined. Place the ears at the top of the hood back piece 10 cm/4 inches apart and evenly placed on each side of the centre hood seam. Baste in place.

6. With right sides together, pin and sew the front hood to the back hood. Follow the notches marked on the pattern to ensure the correct edges are sewn together. Repeat the hood assembly for the lining; without including the ears.

7. Now create the face, attach the pre-cut template pieces to the front hood using a zig zag stitch set on a short stitch length. Attach in the following order:
• Stitch the pupil onto the eye.
• Stitch the eyes onto the front hood, evenly positioned apart from the centre.

8. Now create the trunk. With right sides together, pin and sew around the curved edge of the trunk, then trim the seam to 6 mm/$^1/_4$ inch. Turn the trunk right side out and stuff loosely with fibrefill. Baste the trunk to the centre of the front hood, tucking in the ends as you go to help retain the circular shape.

9. Sew the hood and lining together following the assembly instructions for Version B, Step 3. Sew the hood to the body following the assembly instructions for Version B, Step 4.

10. Sew the front facing following the assembly instructions for Version B, Step 5. Insert the sleeves following the assembly instructions for Version A, Step 5.

11. Follow Steps 7–11 from the assembly instructions for Version A to finish the seams, attach the ribbing and create the buttonholes.

Giraffe

The Giraffe onesie came to life after I found its stunning fabric. Try to locate a similar fabric for your own design as it really makes the style work. This is another perfect character to add to your personal zoo.

Cutting

The fabric requirements are listed in the measurement chart on pages 8–9. Use the pattern pieces from Version B, together with additional pieces from the Giraffe template page:

Ears: Cut 1 pair from the main fabric, and one pair in contrast.
Horn Tip: Cut 2 pairs from brown fabric.
Horn: Cut 2 pairs from the main fabric.
Tail: Cut 1 from the main fabric.

Cut the front insert in contrast fabric. Cut the hood lining pieces from a second contrast fabric. This can be the same colour as the contrast, but try to use a lighter weight fabric than the front insert to avoid too much bulk at the neck seam.

You will also need a small amount of fibrefill for the horns.

Assembly

All the seam allowances are 1.5 cm/⅝ inch.

1.   Baste and sew a piece of brown fur (or similar) onto the tail end. Fold the tail in half lengthwise and with right sides together sew the long raw edges. Leave one end open. Trim the corners and turn the tail through to right side.

fold

Creating a face

As the main fabric is patterned I have not created a face. However, if you wish to add eyes or a nose then refer to 'Create the Face' section from another similar design.

2.   Position the tail on the right side of the centre back seam, 23 cm/9 inches up from the crotch, and baste in place.

3.   For the centre back seam, follow the assembly instructions for Version A, Step 1. For the front insert, follow the assembly instructions for Version B, Step 1. For the shoulder seams, follow the assembly instructions for Version A, Step 2.

4.   To assemble the ears, with right sides together, place one piece of the main fabric with one piece of the contrast fabric. Pin and sew around the curved edges leaving the straight edges open. Trim the seam to 6 mm/¼ inch and turn right side out. Create a 1.2 cm/ ½ inch fold in the ear and baste in place.

5.   Now create the horns. With right sides together, pin and sew the horn tip to

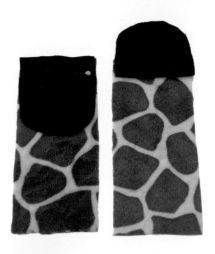

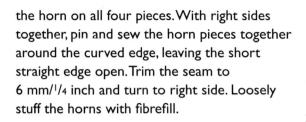

the horn on all four pieces. With right sides together, pin and sew the horn pieces together around the curved edge, leaving the short straight edge open. Trim the seam to 6 mm/¹/₄ inch and turn to right side. Loosely stuff the horns with fibrefill.

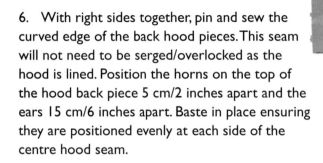

6.   With right sides together, pin and sew the curved edge of the back hood pieces. This seam will not need to be serged/overlocked as the hood is lined. Position the horns on the top of the hood back piece 5 cm/2 inches apart and the ears 15 cm/6 inches apart. Baste in place ensuring they are positioned evenly at each side of the centre hood seam.

7.   With right sides together, pin and sew the front hood to the back hood. Follow the notches marked on the pattern to ensure the correct edges are sewn together. Repeat the hood assembly for the lining, without including the ears and horns.

8.   Sew the hood and lining together following the assembly instructions for Version B, Step 3.
    Sew the hood to the body following the assembly instructions for Version B, Step 4.

9.   Sew the front facing following the assembly instructions for Version B, Step 5. Insert the sleeves following the assembly instructions for Version A, Step 5.

10. Follow Steps 7–11 from the assembly instructions for Version A to finish the seams, attach the ribbing and create the buttonholes.

Superhero

This basic onesie style is transformed into the costume of a fearless superhero with the addition of a simple red cape and some bright stars. It is quick to make and the strong colours look amazing.

Cutting

The fabric requirements are listed in the measurement chart on pages 8–9. Follow the assembly instructions and pattern pieces for Version A, plus additional pieces from the superhero template:

Back star: Cut 1 from white jersey, pre prepared with fusible web

Front Star (white): Cut 1 from white jersey, pre prepared with fusible web

Front Star (red):   Cut 1 from red jersey, pre prepared with fusible web

Cape: Draft the cape pattern following the measurement chart on page 99 and cut 1 in red jersey

In addition you will need:

- Red jersey fabric for the cape (refer to column B in the measurement chart on page 99 for the required amount of fabric).
- 25 cm/10 inches white jersey fabric for the stars.
- 25 cm/10 inches fusible web

Bonding fabrics

If your fabric has a fluffy or raised surface be extremely careful when using the iron to position the stars into place. Use a pressing cloth or rather try to hold the star in place with pins.

Using fusible web

1. Cut a piece of fusible web large enough to cover your desired shape.

2. Iron the rough glue side of the fusible web to the wrong side of your fabric.

3. Cut your shape from this prepared fabric piece

4. Peel the paper from the fabric.

5. Iron the shape onto your garment with the glue side facing down.

Size	A Inches	A cm	B Inches	B cm	C Inches	C cm
2	15 in	38 cm	23½ in	60 cm	23 in	58 cm
4	15¾ in	40 cm	26¾ in	68 cm	23¾ in	60 cm
6	16½ in	42 cm	30 in	76 cm	24½ in	62 cm
8	17¼ in	44 cm	33 in	84 cm	25¼ in	64 cm
10	18 in	46 cm	36¼ in	92 cm	26 in	66 cm

Assembly

All the seam allowances are 1.5 cm/⁵⁄₈ inch.

1. For the centre back seam, follow the assembly instructions for Version A, Step 1.

2. Iron the large white star to the centre of the cape. Zig zag stitch around all the edges.

3. Create a 1.2 cm/¹⁄₂ inch hem on the two long sides of the cape and the bottom edge. Place the raw top edge of the cape onto the back neckline and cut the cape neckline to match the onesie neckline shape. Baste the cape to the shoulder and neckline.

4. Create the front star. Iron the larger white star to the left front chest, then iron the smaller red star on top. Zig zag stitch around all edges of both star shapes.

5. Complete the onesie by following Steps 2–11 of the assembly instructions for Version A. When inserting the sleeves, be careful not to catch the cape into the armhole seam.

Hearts

This gorgeous Heart onesie is easy and quick to make. I especially love the heart motif on the bottom, and its pretty mix of colours. With no limit to fabric choices it's the perfect everyday onesie.

Cutting

The fabric requirements are listed in the measurement chart on pages 8–9. Refer to the pattern pieces and assembly instructions for Version A, together with additional pieces from the Hearts template page:

Heart pockets: Cut 4 from jersey, and 2 from stabilising fabric.

Back heart: Cut 1 from jersey that has been pre prepared with fusible web

In addition you will need:
- 30 cm/12 inches contrast jersey fabric for the hearts.
- 30 cm/12 inches fusible web.
- 18 cm/7 inches iron-on stabilising fabric.

103

Assembly

All the seam allowances are 1.5 cm/⅝ inch.

1. For the centre back seam follow the assembly instructions for Version A, Step 1.

2. Now attach the back heart. Position the large back heart on the centre back seam, approximately 7.5 cm/ 3 inches up from the crotch. Iron into place then zig zag stitch around the raw edges.

3. Next, create the heart pockets. Iron the stabilising fabric onto the back of two of the heart pieces. Take one heart piece that is stabilised and one that is not and place with right sides together. Sew around all the edges, but leave a 4 cm/1½ inches opening on the straight section. Trim the seam to 6 mm/¼ inch around the curved part of the heart and clip into the corner. Turn to the right side and tuck the edges of the opening inside the heart so that it can be closed up when you attach the heart pockets.

4. To determine the pocket position, refer to the chart below. Attach the pocket to the front by edge stitching around the pocket edges, leaving the top section open.

Distance from shoulder to pocket		
Size	cm	inches
2	32 cm	12½ in
4	36 cm	14 in
6	39 cm	15½ in
8	43 cm	17 in
10	47 cm	18½ in

Using fusible web

1. Cut a piece of fusible web large enough to cover your desired shape.

2. Iron the rough glue side of the fusible web to the wrong side of your fabric.

3. Cut your shape from this prepared fabric piece

4. Peel the paper from the fabric.

5. Iron the shape onto your garment with the glue side facing down.

5. For the shoulder seams, follow the assembly instructions for Version A, Step 2.

6. For the hood seam, follow the assembly instructions for Version A, Step 3, and repeat for the lining.

7. Next sew the hood to the lining. With right sides together pin the long edge of the front hood main fabric to the front hood lining fabric. Sew, using a 2.5 cm/1 inch seam allowance, then trim it to 1.5 cm/$5/8$ inch. Turn the hood right side out and topstitch along this edge to stop the lining from rolling out of place.

8. Baste the hood and lining together around the neckline edge. This will make sewing the hood to the body easier.

9. Now sew the hood to the body, following the assembly instructions for Version B, Step 4. Then sew the front facing following the assembly instructions for Version B, Step 5.

10. To insert the sleeves, follow the assembly instructions for Version A, Step 5.

11. Follow Steps 7–11 from the assembly instructions for Version A to finish the seams, attach the ribbing and create the buttonholes

If your fabric has a fluffy or raised surface be extremely careful when using the iron to position the heart into place. Use a pressing cloth, or hold the heart in place with pins.

Templates

Onesie Version A + B

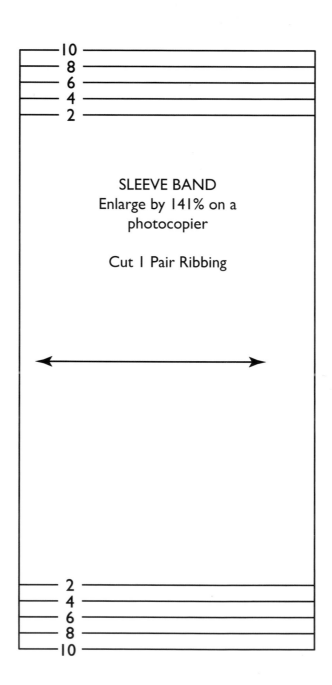

10

8

6

4

2

SLEEVE BAND
Enlarge by 141% on a
photocopier

Cut 1 Pair Ribbing

2

4

6

8

10

Onesie Version A + B

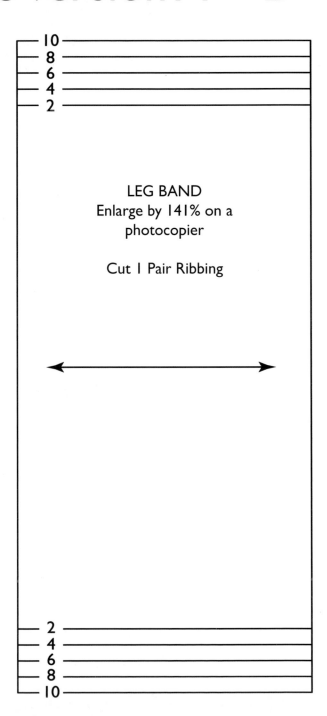

10
8
6
4
2

LEG BAND
Enlarge by 141% on a
photocopier

Cut 1 Pair Ribbing

2
4
6
8
10

Onesie Version A + B

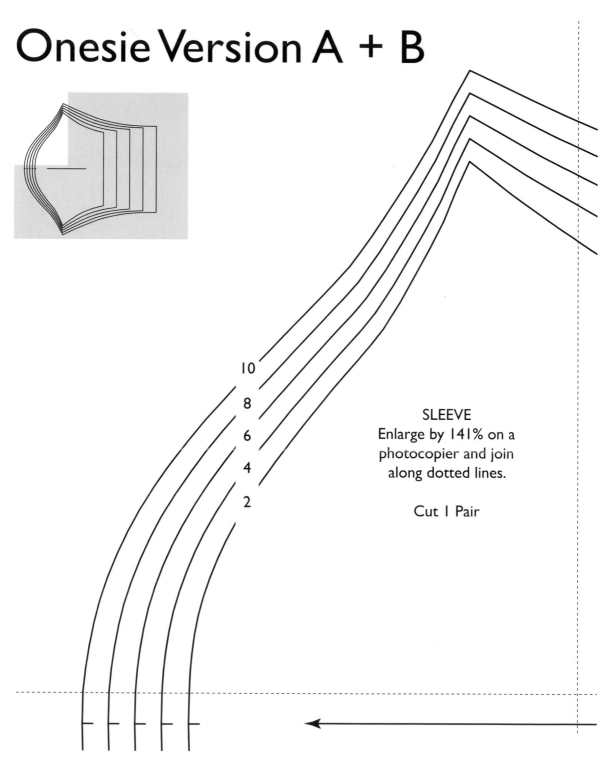

10

8

6

4

2

SLEEVE
Enlarge by 141% on a
photocopier and join
along dotted lines.

Cut 1 Pair

Onesie Version A + B

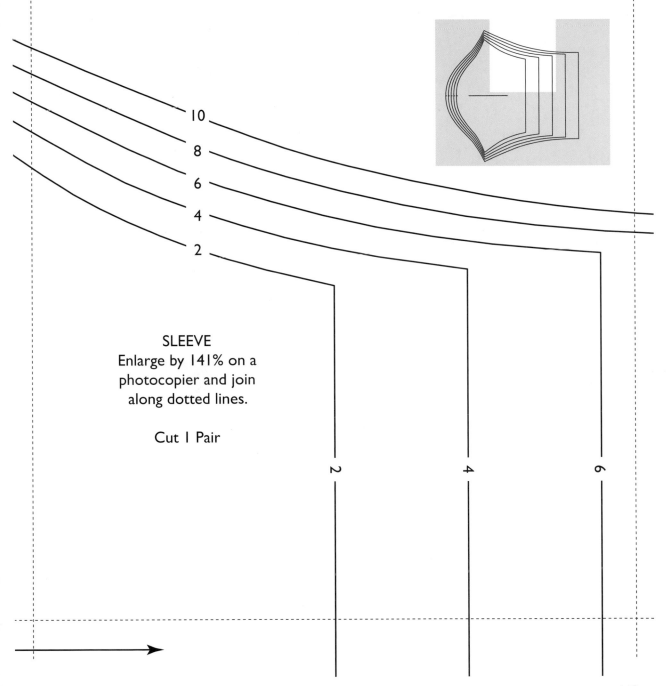

10

8

6

4

2

SLEEVE
Enlarge by 141% on a
photocopier and join
along dotted lines.

Cut 1 Pair

2

4

6

Onesie Version A + B

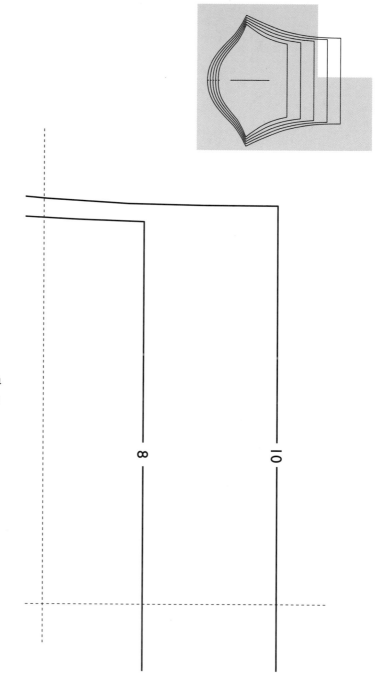

SLEEVE
Enlarge by 141% on a photocopier and join along dotted lines.

Cut 1 Pair

8

10

Onesie Version A + B

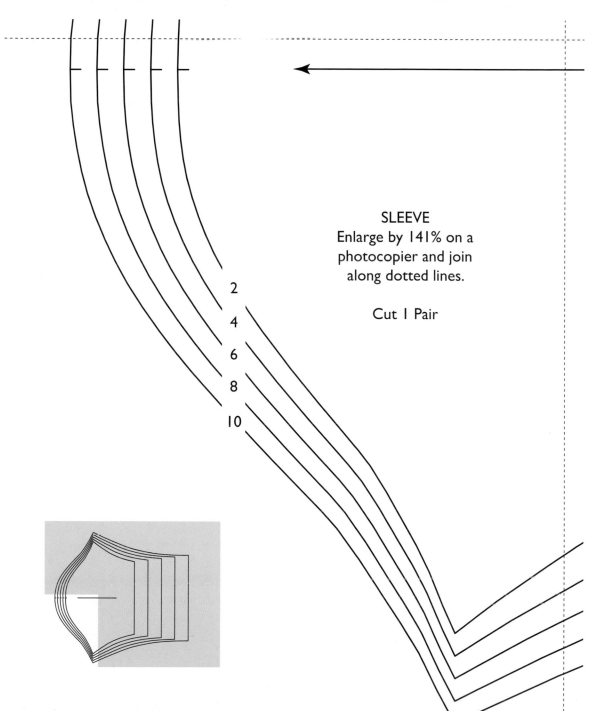

2

4

6

8

10

SLEEVE
Enlarge by 141% on a
photocopier and join
along dotted lines.

Cut 1 Pair

Onesie Version A + B

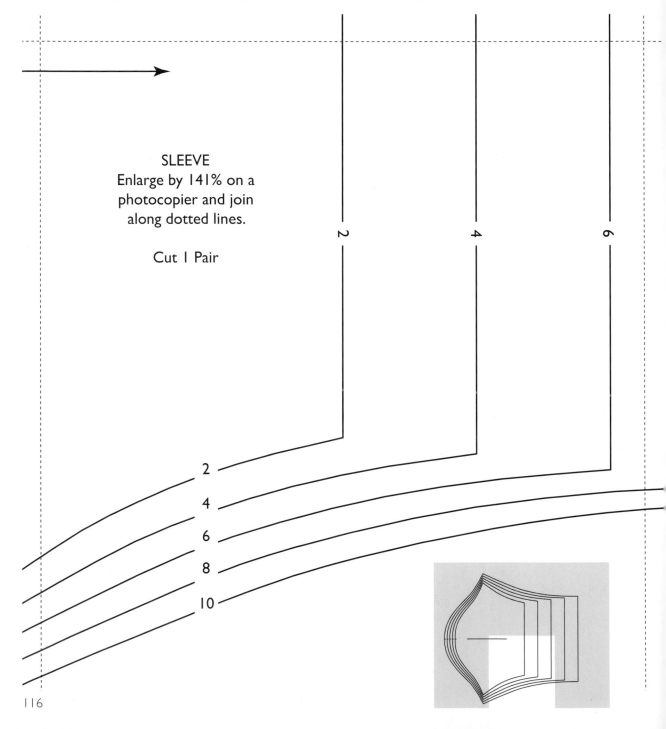

SLEEVE
Enlarge by 141% on a
photocopier and join
along dotted lines.

Cut 1 Pair

2

4

6

2

4

6

8

10

Onesie Version A + B

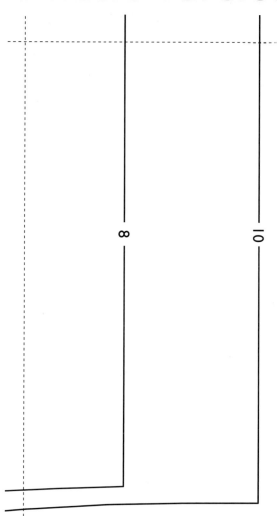

8

10

SLEEVE
Enlarge by 141% on a
photocopier and join
along dotted lines.

Cut 1 Pair

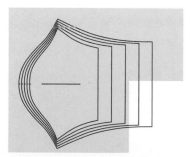

Onesie Version A

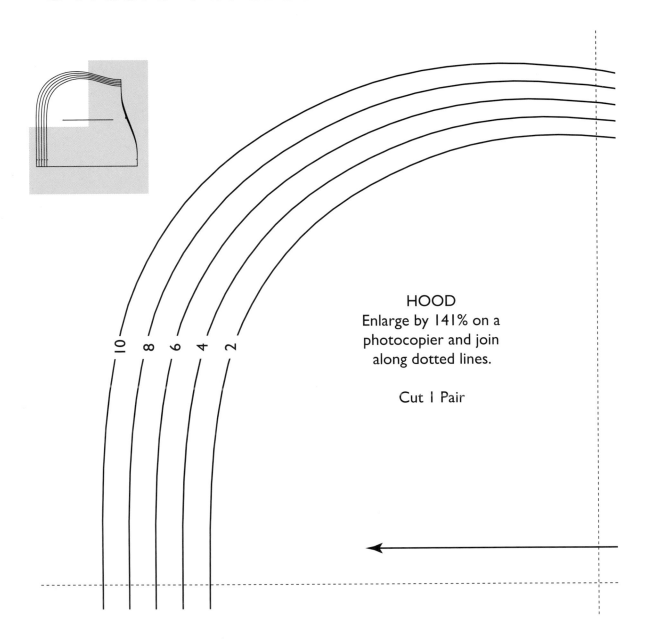

10   8   6   4   2

HOOD
Enlarge by 141% on a
photocopier and join
along dotted lines.

Cut 1 Pair

Onesie Version A

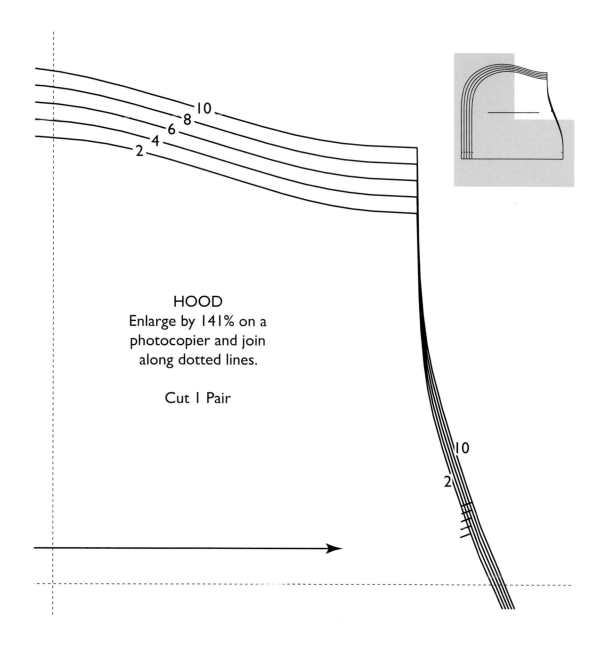

10
8
6
4
2

HOOD
Enlarge by 141% on a
photocopier and join
along dotted lines.

Cut 1 Pair

10
2

Onesie Version A

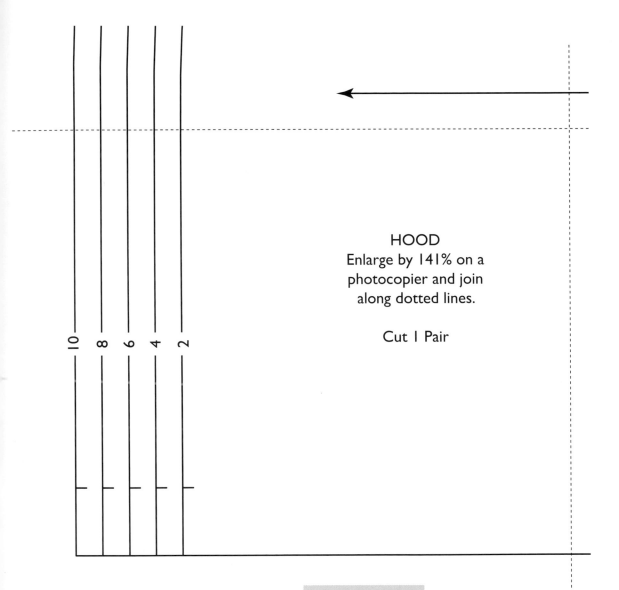

10 8 6 4 2

HOOD
Enlarge by 141% on a
photocopier and join
along dotted lines.

Cut 1 Pair

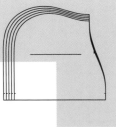

Onesie Version A

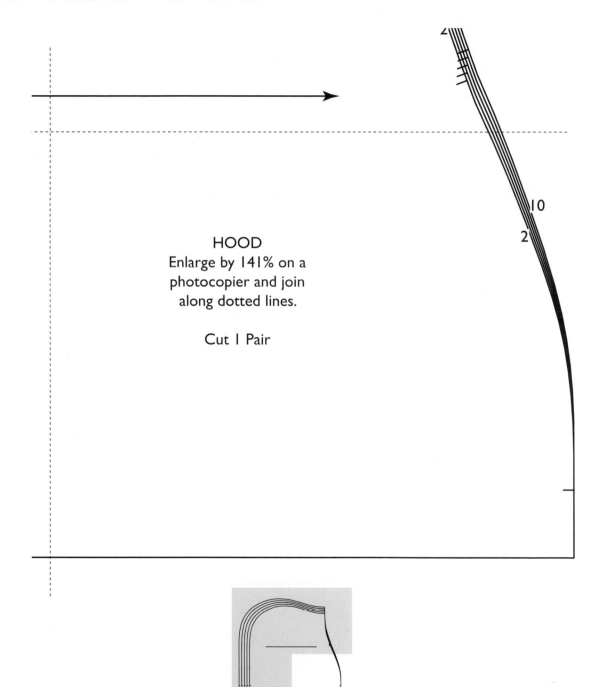

HOOD
Enlarge by 141% on a
photocopier and join
along dotted lines.

Cut 1 Pair

2

10

2

Onesie Version B

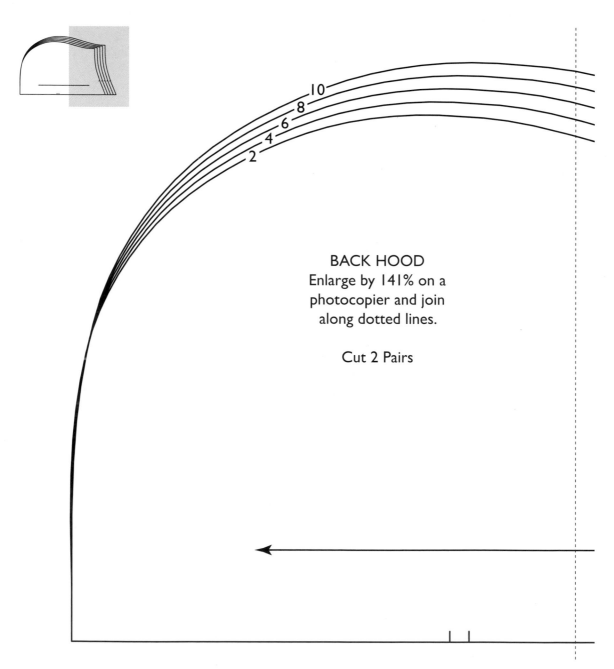

10
2 4 6 8

BACK HOOD
Enlarge by 141% on a
photocopier and join
along dotted lines.

Cut 2 Pairs

Onesie Version B

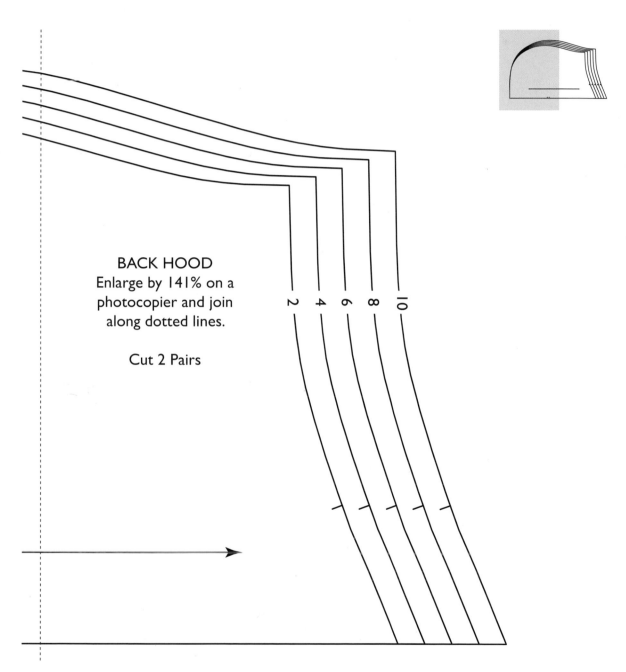

BACK HOOD
Enlarge by 141% on a
photocopier and join
along dotted lines.

Cut 2 Pairs

2

4

6

8

10

Onesie Version B

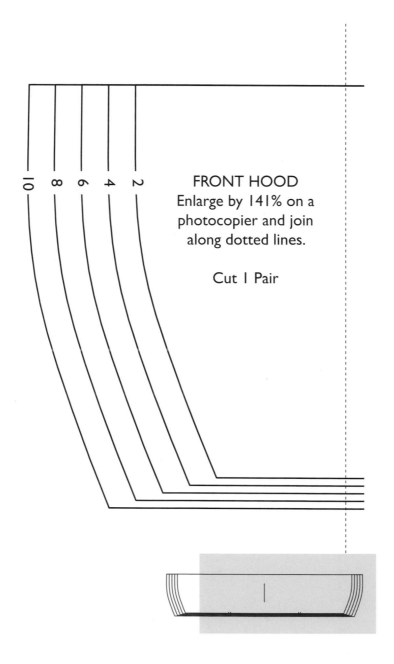

10 8 6 4 2

FRONT HOOD
Enlarge by 141% on a
photocopier and join
along dotted lines.

Cut 1 Pair

Onesie Version B

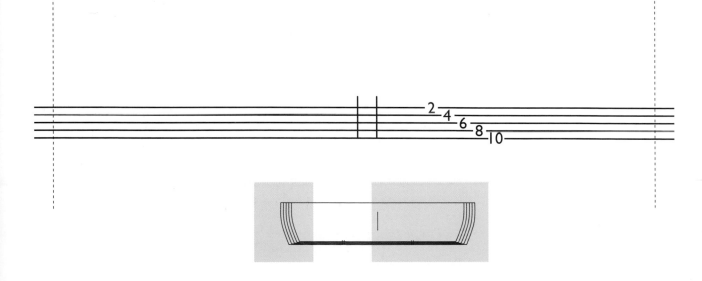

FRONT HOOD
Enlarge by 141% on a
photocopier and join
along dotted lines.

Cut 1 Pair

2
4
6
8
10

Onesie Version B

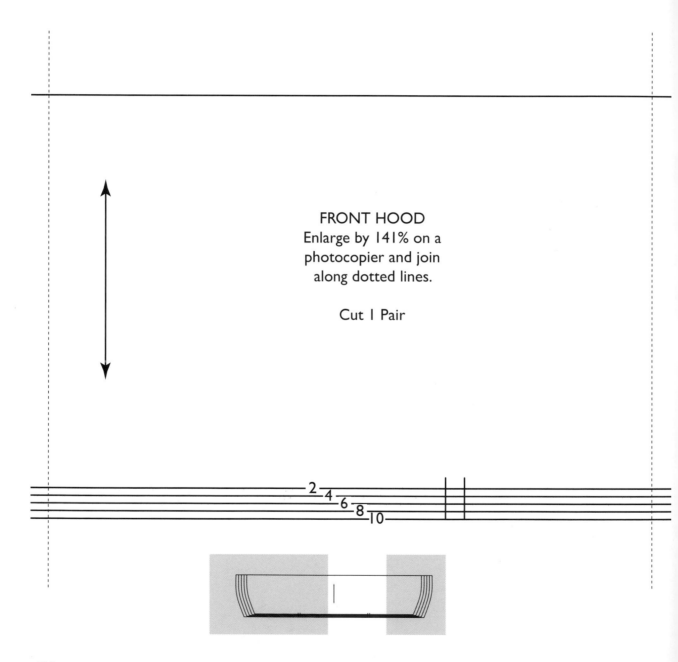

FRONT HOOD
Enlarge by 141% on a
photocopier and join
along dotted lines.

Cut 1 Pair

2
4
6
8
10

Onesie Version B

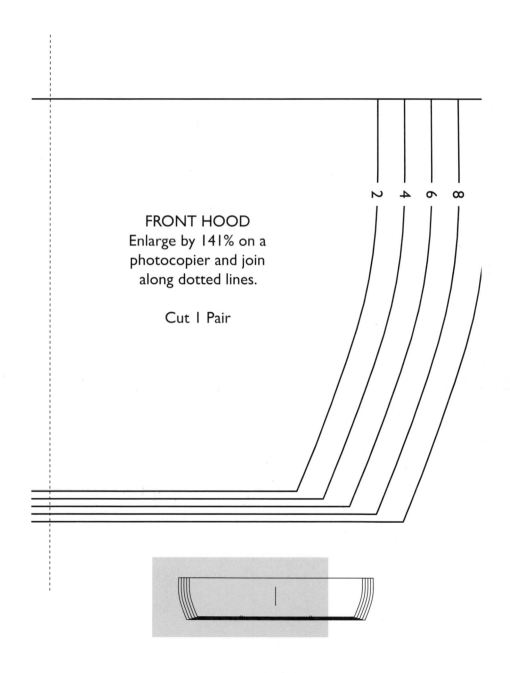

FRONT HOOD
Enlarge by 141% on a
photocopier and join
along dotted lines.

Cut 1 Pair

2 4 6 8

Onesie Version B

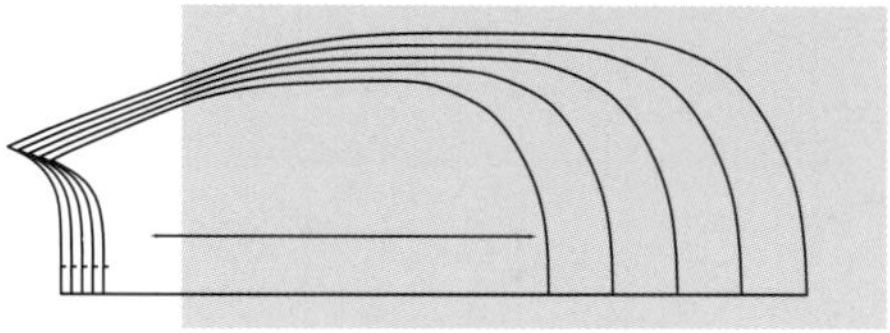

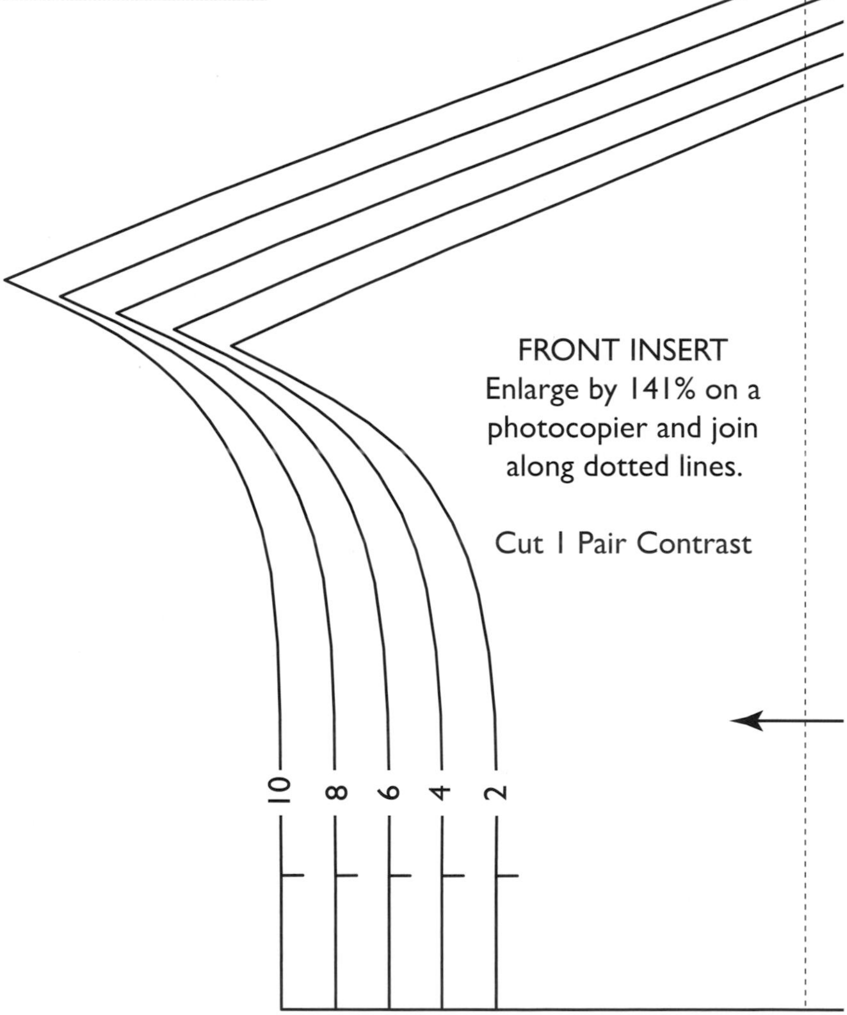

FRONT INSERT
Enlarge by 141% on a
photocopier and join
along dotted lines.

Cut 1 Pair Contrast

10   8   6   4   2

Onesie Version B

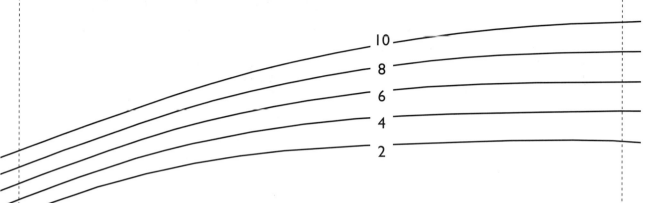

10
8
6
4
2

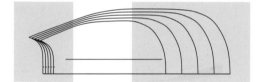

FRONT INSERT
Enlarge by 141% on a
photocopier and join
along dotted lines.

Cut 1 Pair Contrast

Onesie Version B

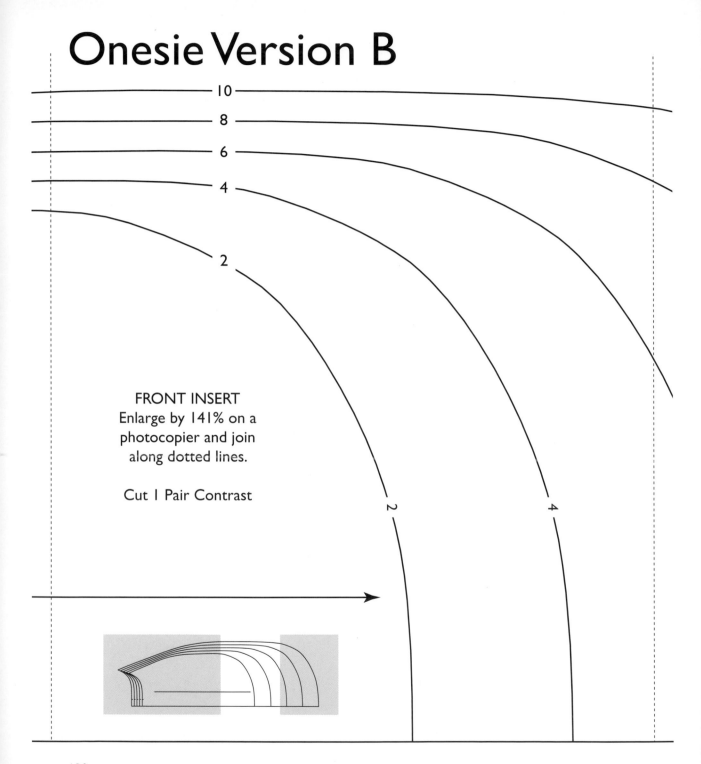

10

8

6

4

2

2

4

FRONT INSERT
Enlarge by 141% on a
photocopier and join
along dotted lines.

Cut 1 Pair Contrast

Onesie Version B

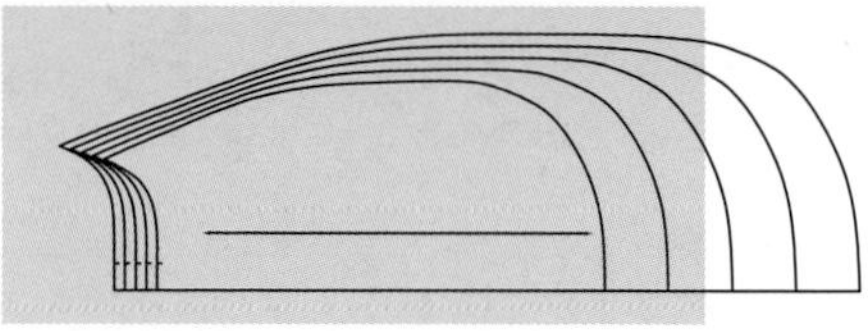

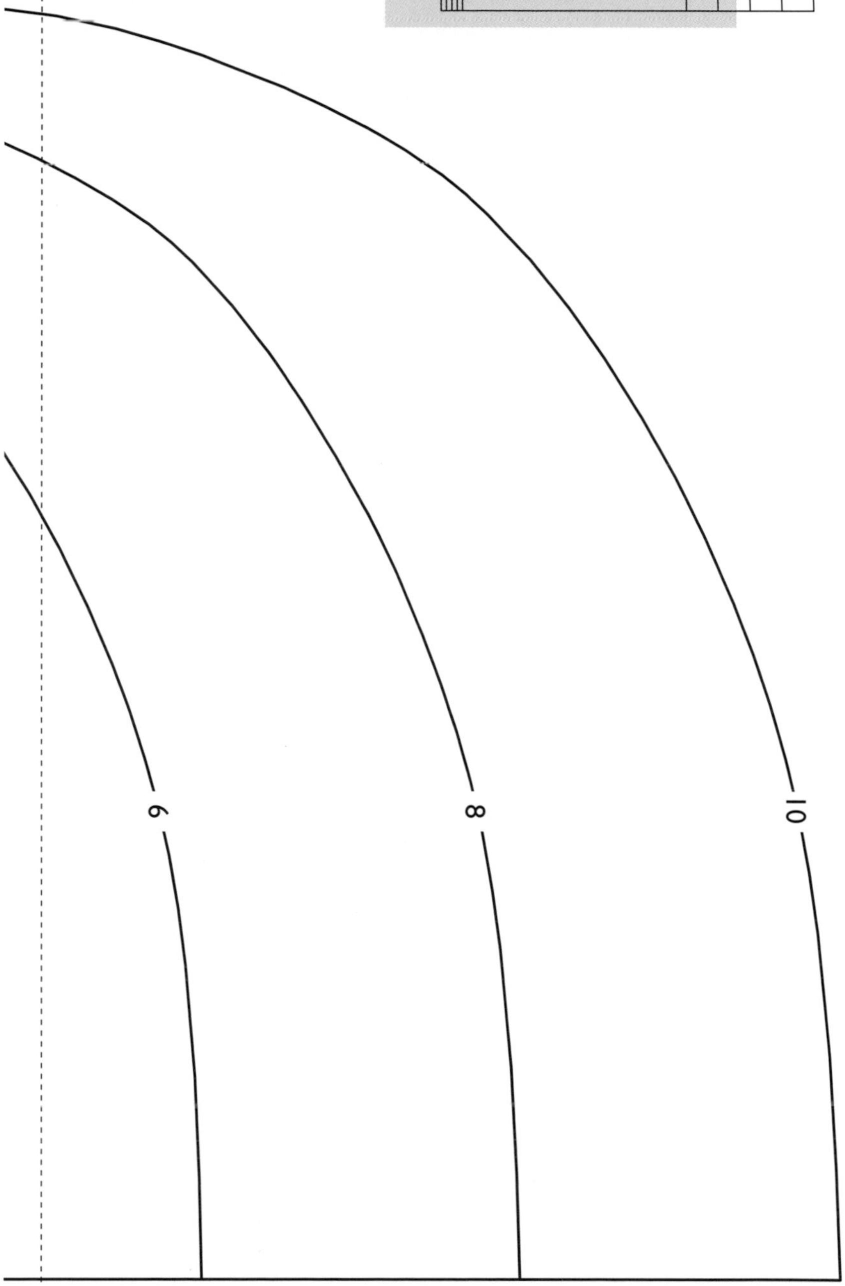

FRONT INSERT
Enlarge by 141% on a
photocopier and join
along dotted lines.

Cut 1 Pair Contrast

6

8

10

Onesie Version A

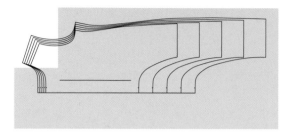

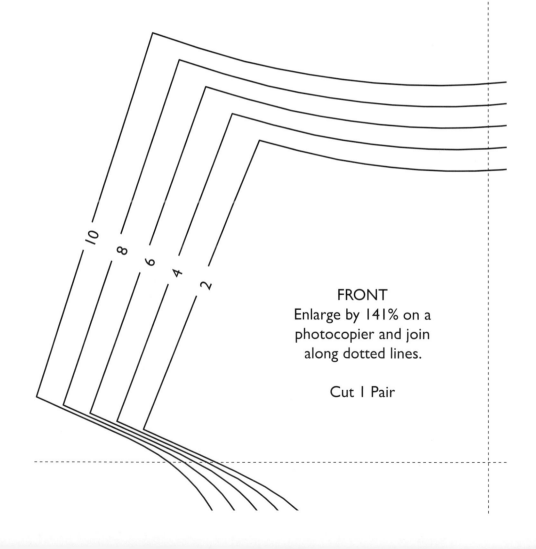

10

8

6

4

2

FRONT
Enlarge by 141% on a
photocopier and join
along dotted lines.

Cut 1 Pair

Onesie Version A

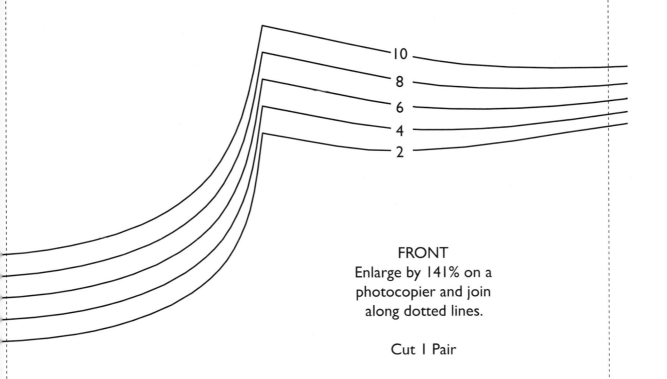

10
8
6
4
2

FRONT
Enlarge by 141% on a
photocopier and join
along dotted lines.

Cut 1 Pair

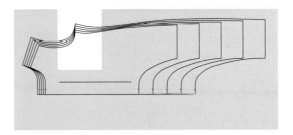

Onesie Version A

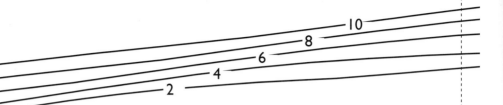

FRONT
Enlarge by 141% on a
photocopier and join
along dotted lines.

Cut 1 Pair

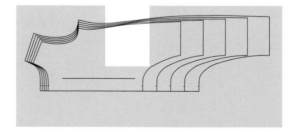

Onesie Version A

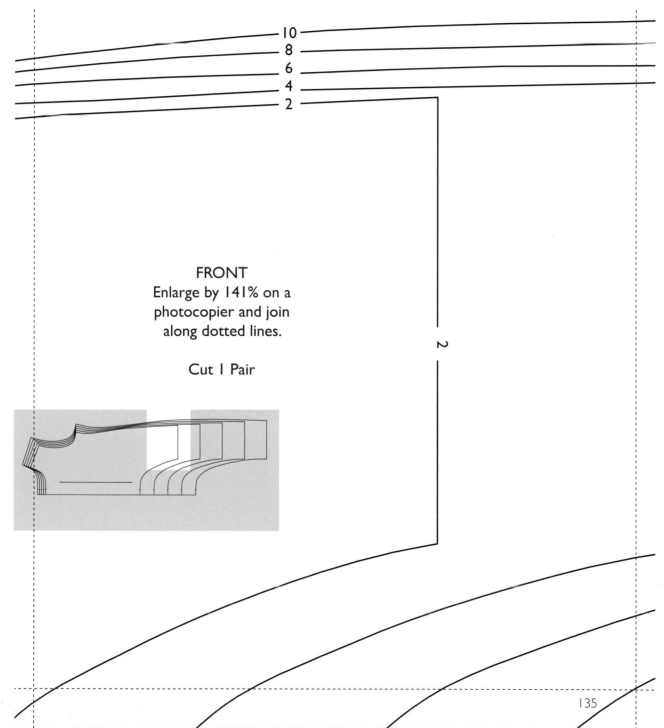

10
8
6
4
2

FRONT
Enlarge by 141% on a
photocopier and join
along dotted lines.

Cut 1 Pair

2

Onesie Version A

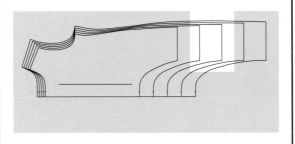

4

6

FRONT
Enlarge by 141% on a
photocopier and join
along dotted lines.

Cut 1 Pair

Onesie Version A

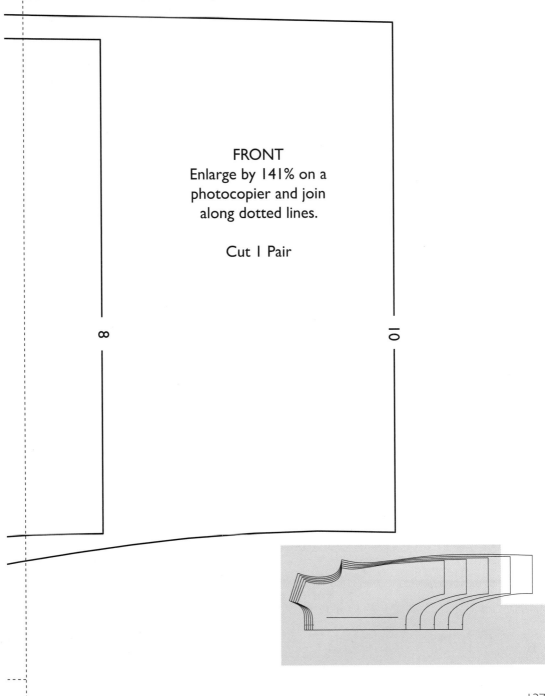

FRONT
Enlarge by 141% on a
photocopier and join
along dotted lines.

Cut 1 Pair

8

10

Onesie Version A

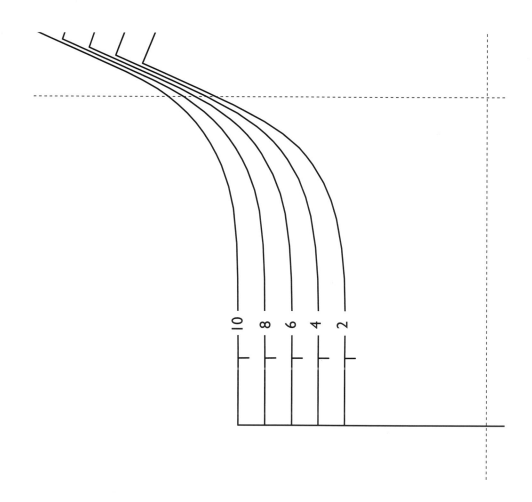

10 8 6 4 2

FRONT
Enlarge by 141% on a
photocopier and join
along dotted lines.

Cut 1 Pair

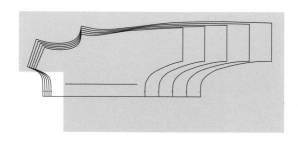

Onesie Version A

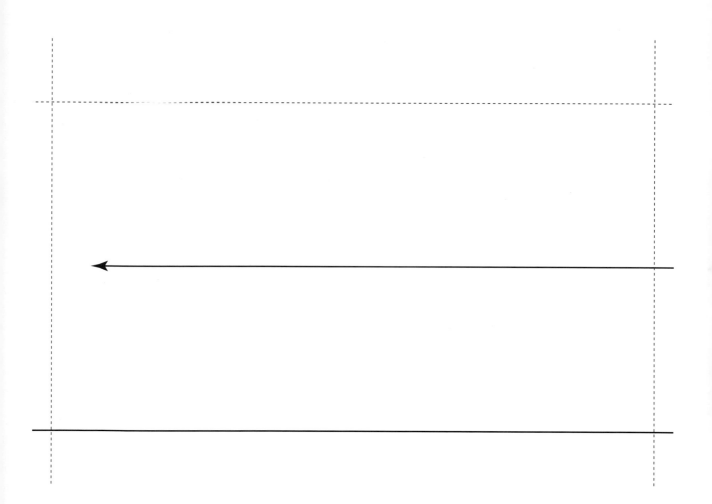

FRONT
Enlarge by 141% on a
photocopier and join
along dotted lines.

Cut 1 Pair

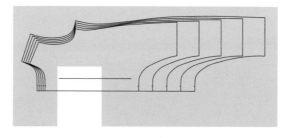

Onesie Version A

FRONT
Enlarge by 141% on a
photocopier and join
along dotted lines.

Cut 1 Pair

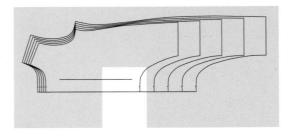

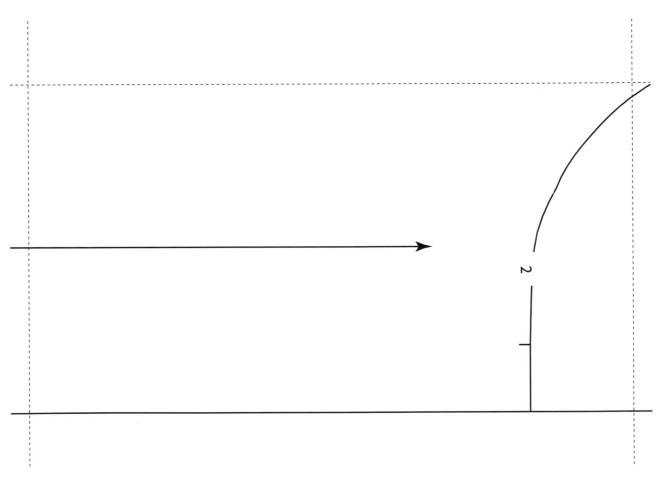

Onesie Version A

FRONT
Enlarge by 141% on a
photocopier and join
along dotted lines.

Cut 1 Pair

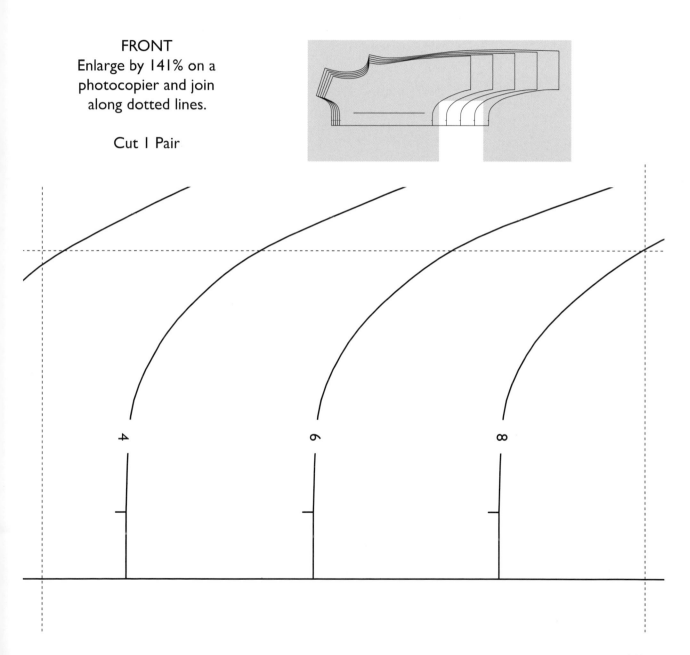

4

6

8

Onesie Version A

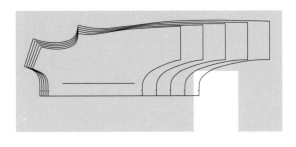

10

FRONT
Enlarge by 141% on a
photocopier and join
along dotted lines.

Cut 1 Pair

Onesie Version B

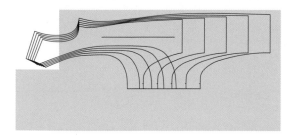

FRONT
Enlarge by 141% on a
photocopier and join
along dotted lines.

Cut 1 Pair

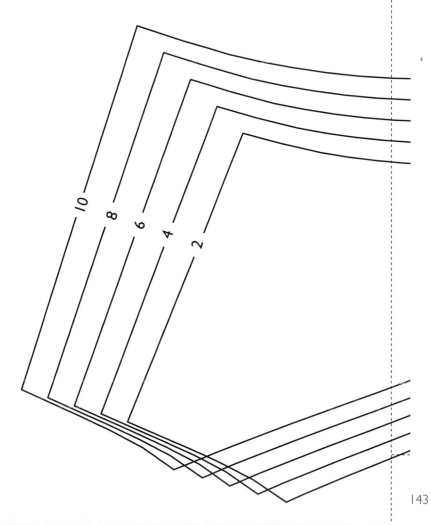

10
8
6
4
2

Onesie Version B

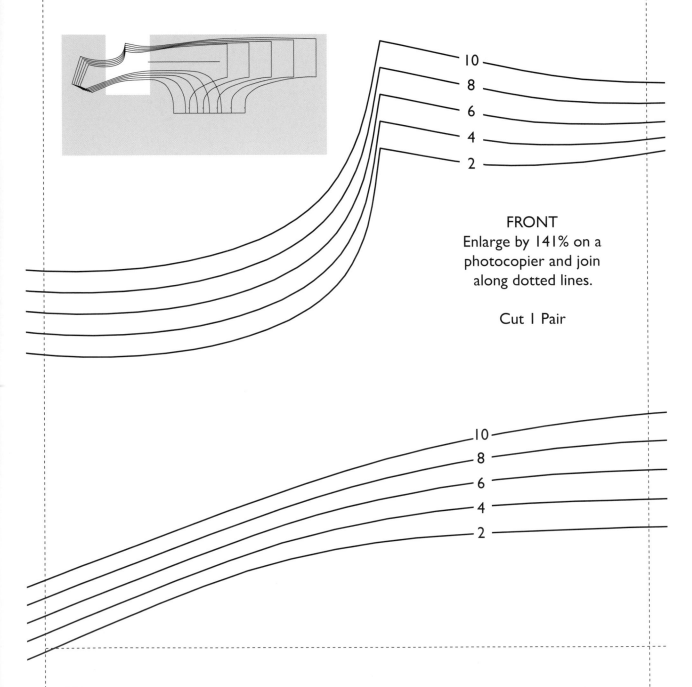

10
8
6
4
2

FRONT
Enlarge by 141% on a
photocopier and join
along dotted lines.

Cut 1 Pair

10
8
6
4
2

Onesie Version B

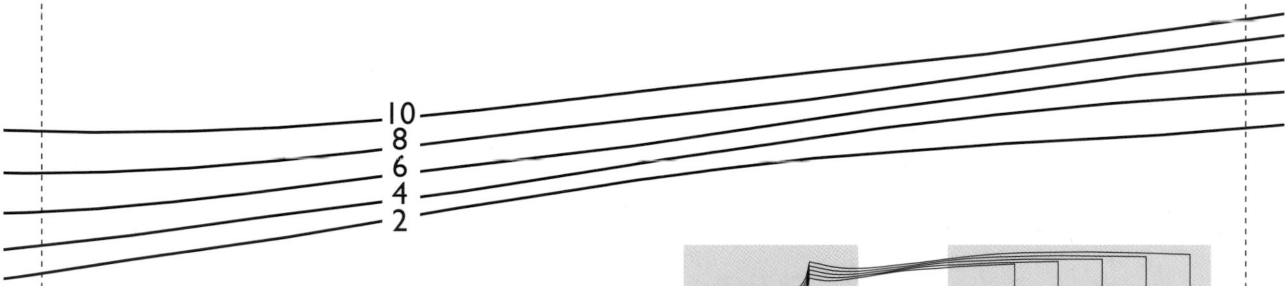

10
8
6
4
2

FRONT
Enlarge by 141% on a
photocopier and join
along dotted lines.

Cut 1 Pair

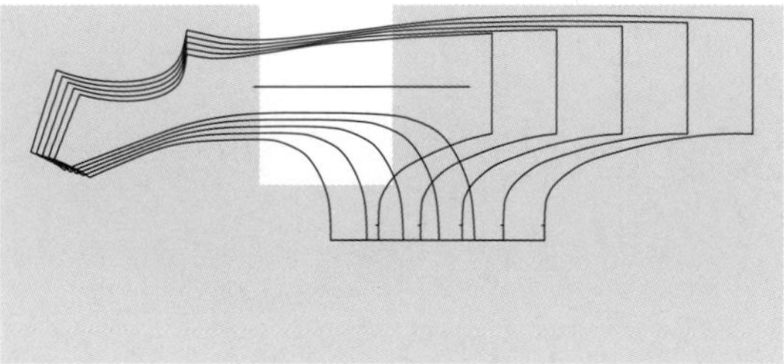

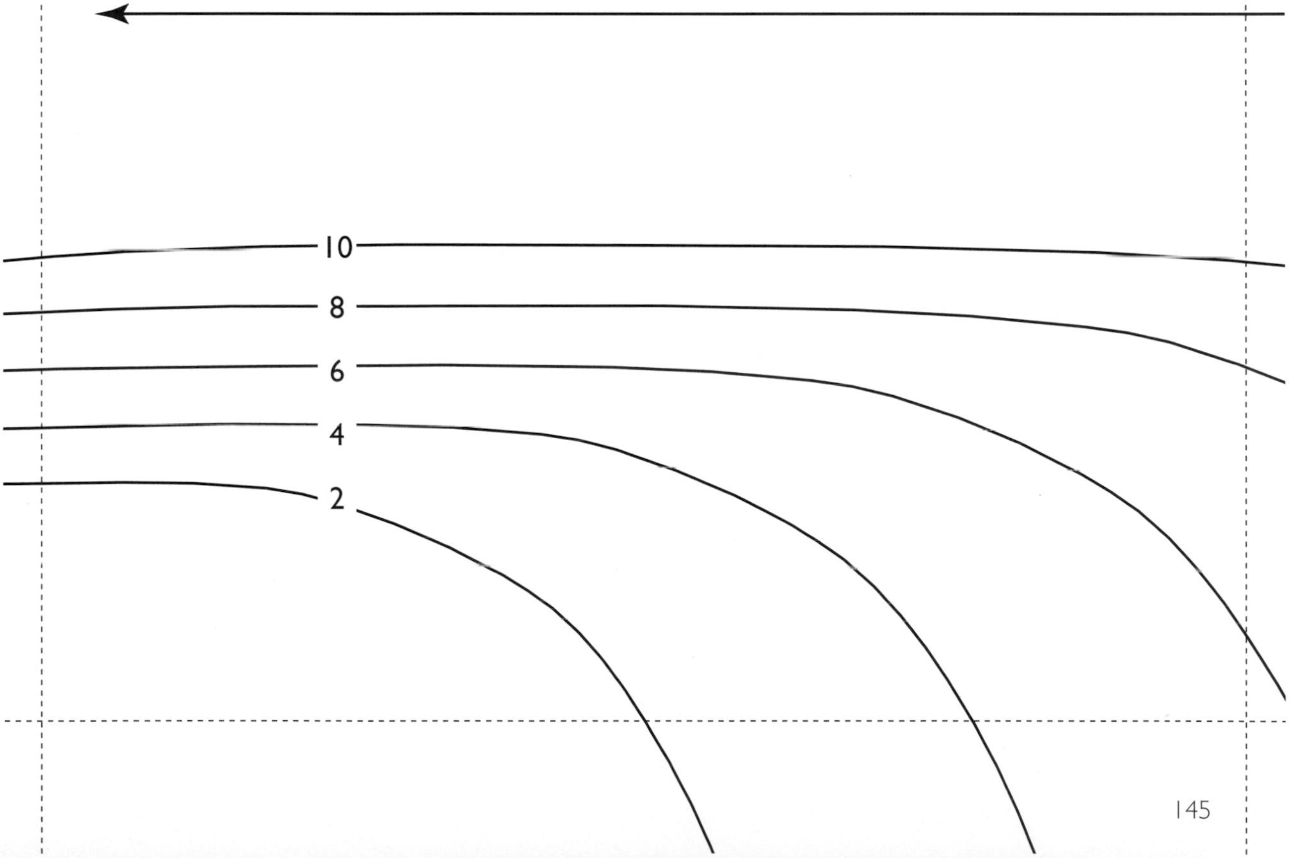

10

8

6

4

2

Onesie Version B

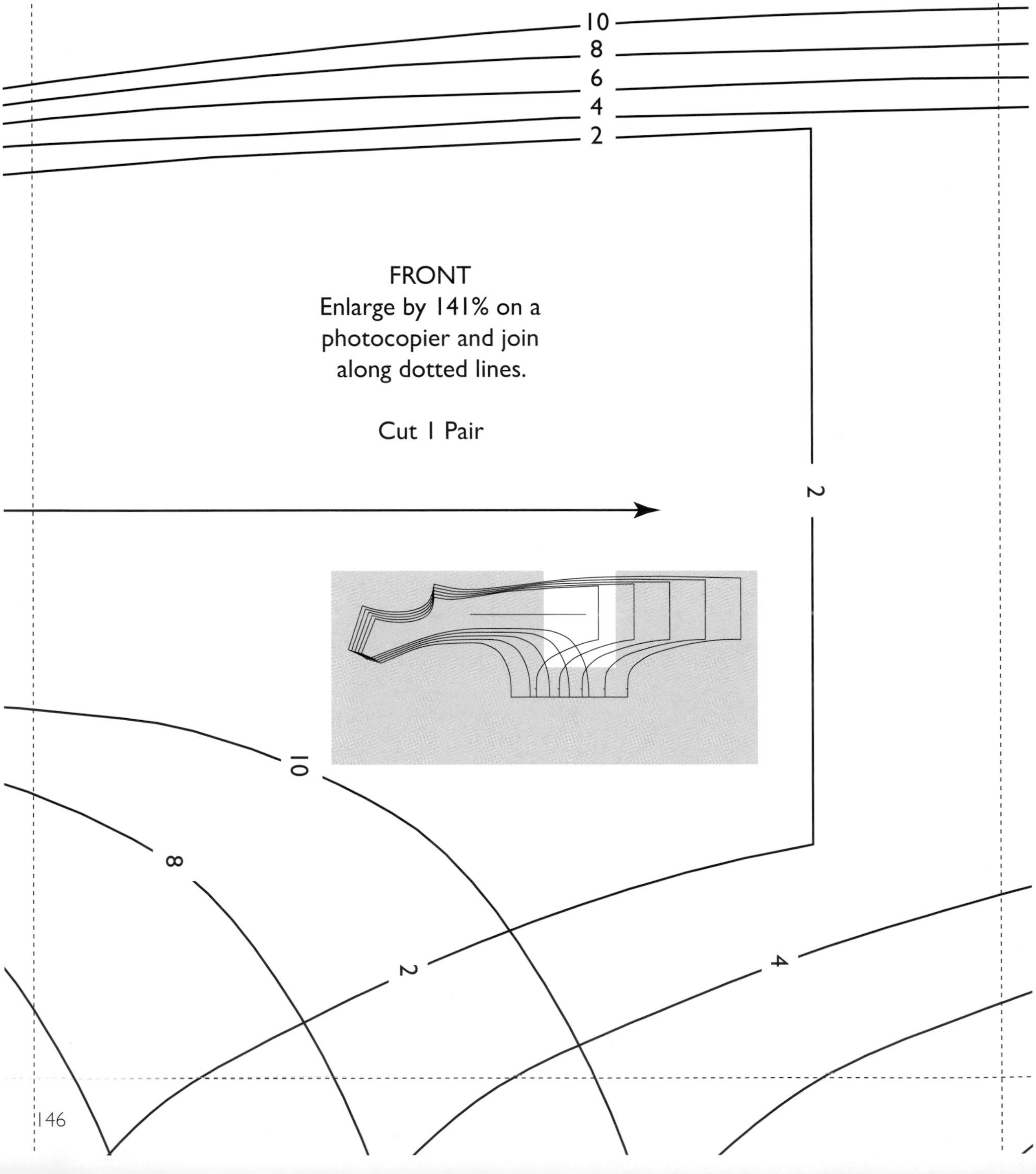

10
8
6
4
2

FRONT
Enlarge by 141% on a
photocopier and join
along dotted lines.

Cut 1 Pair

2

2

10

8

2

4

146

Onesie Version B

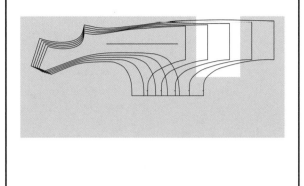

4

6

FRONT
Enlarge by 141% on a
photocopier and join
along dotted lines.

Cut 1 Pair

Onesie Version B

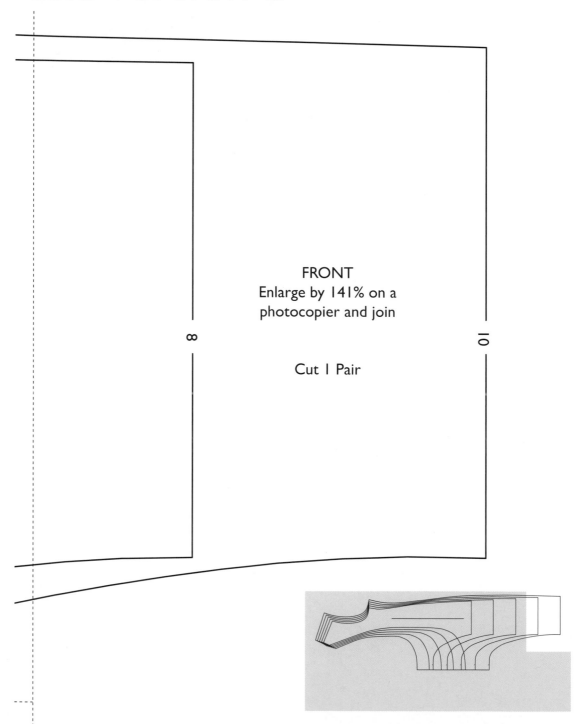

FRONT
Enlarge by 141% on a
photocopier and join

Cut 1 Pair

8

10

Onesie Version B

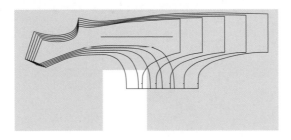

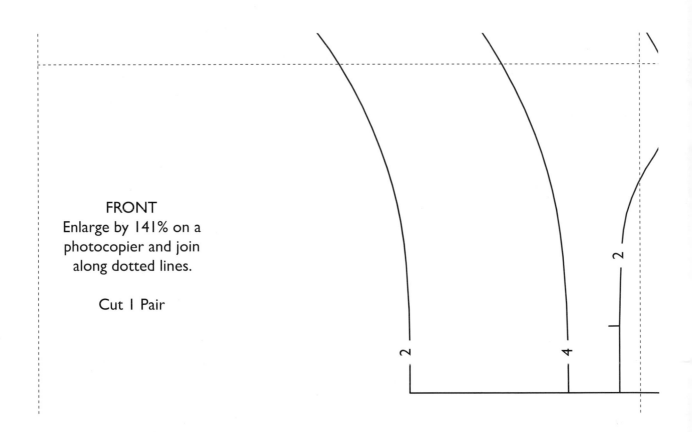

FRONT
Enlarge by 141% on a
photocopier and join
along dotted lines.

Cut 1 Pair

2

4

2

Onesie Version B

FRONT
Enlarge by 141% on a
photocopier and join
along dotted lines.

Cut 1 Pair

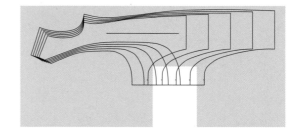

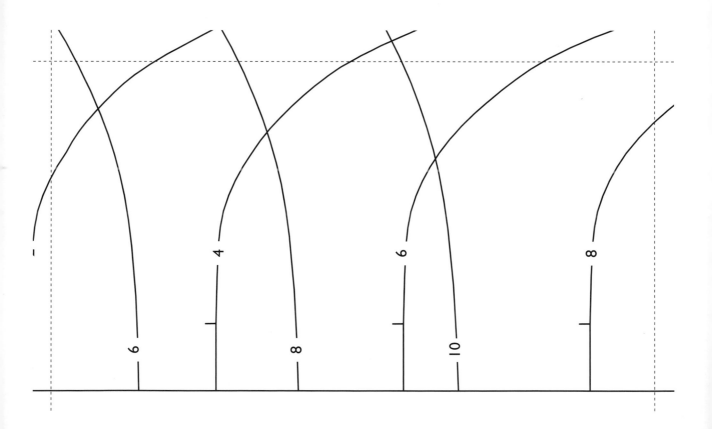

Onesie Version B

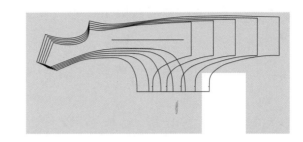

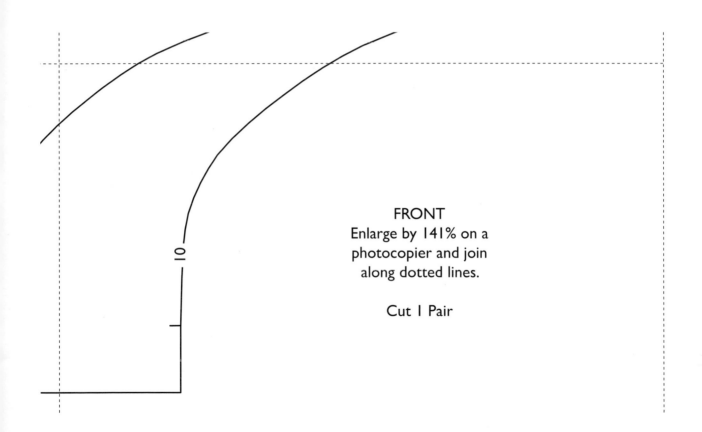

FRONT
Enlarge by 141% on a
photocopier and join
along dotted lines.

Cut 1 Pair

10

Onesie Version A+B

BACK
Enlarge by 141% on a
photocopier and join
along dotted lines.

Cut 1 Pair

10

8

6

4

2

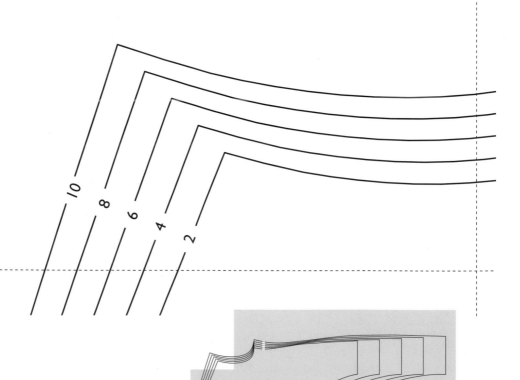

Onesie Version A+B

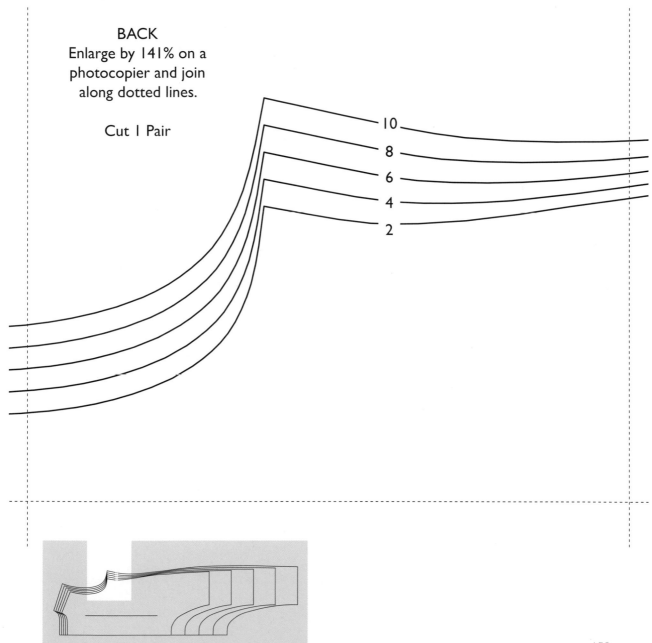

BACK
Enlarge by 141% on a
photocopier and join
along dotted lines.

Cut 1 Pair

10

8

6

4

2

Onesie Version A+B

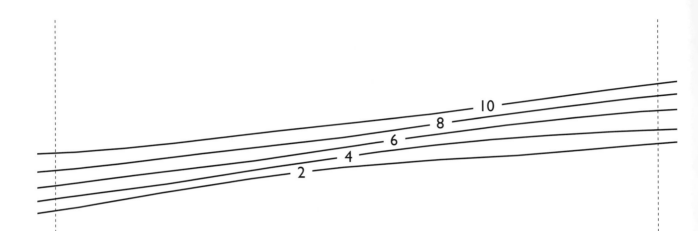

10

8

6

4

2

BACK
Enlarge by 141% on a
photocopier and join
along dotted lines.

Cut 1 Pair

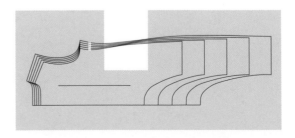

Onesie Version A+B

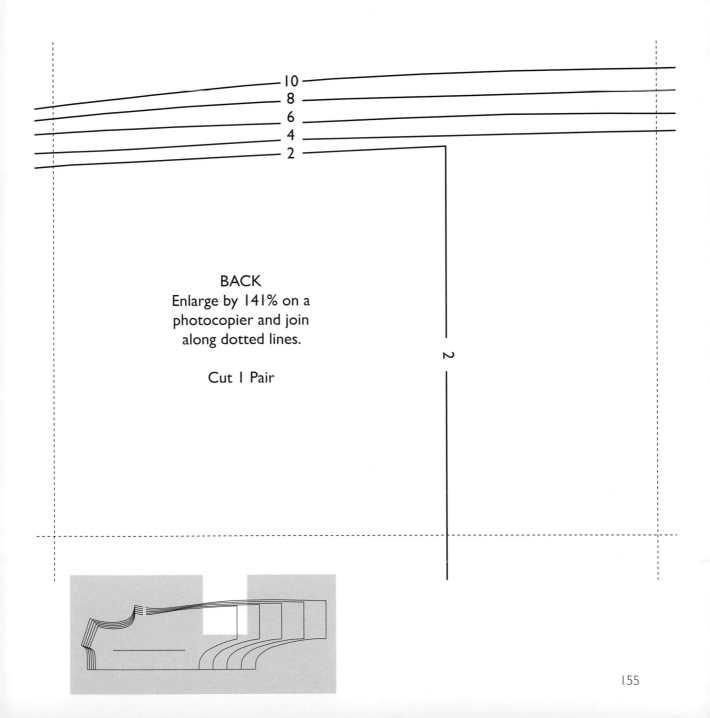

10
8
6
4
2

BACK
Enlarge by 141% on a
photocopier and join
along dotted lines.

Cut 1 Pair

2

Onesie Version A+B

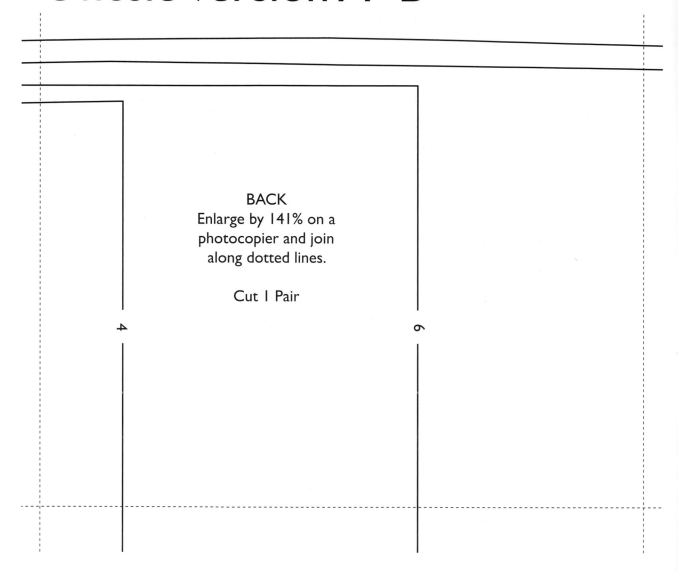

BACK
Enlarge by 141% on a
photocopier and join
along dotted lines.

Cut 1 Pair

4

6

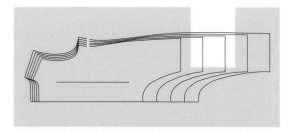

Onesie Version A+B

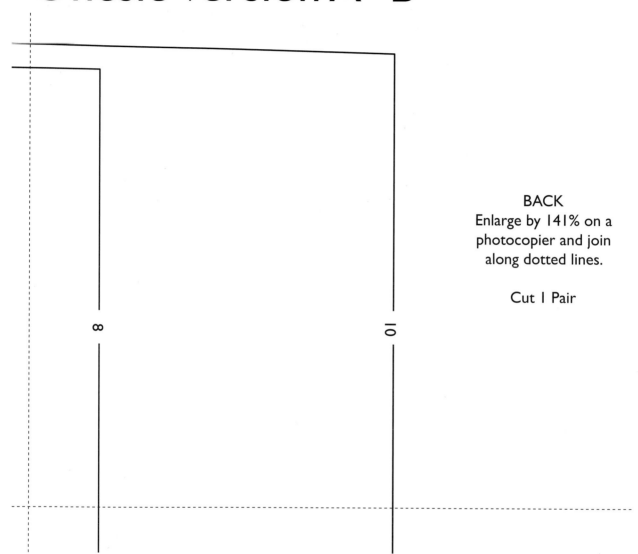

8

10

BACK
Enlarge by 141% on a
photocopier and join
along dotted lines.

Cut 1 Pair

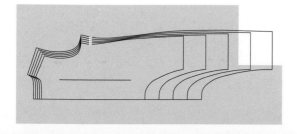

Onesie Version A+B

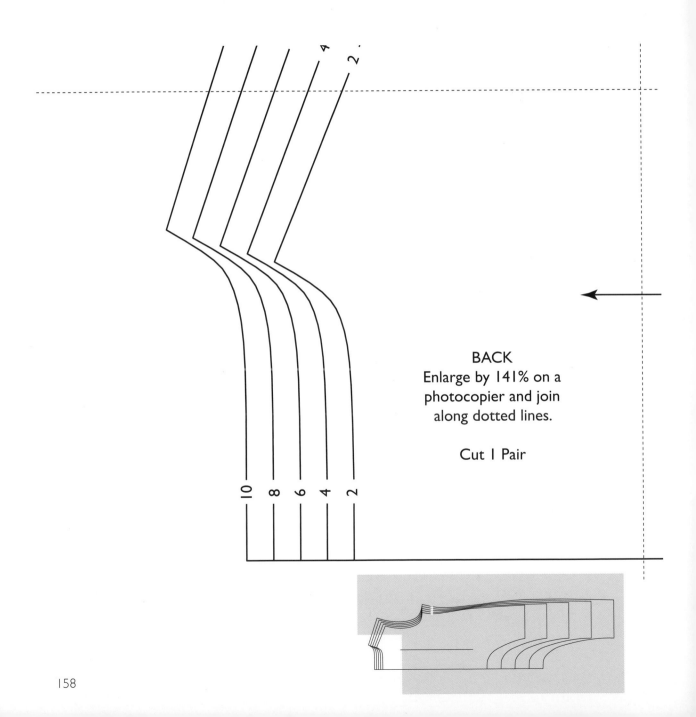

4
2

BACK
Enlarge by 141% on a
photocopier and join
along dotted lines.

Cut 1 Pair

10 8 6 4 2

Onesie Version A+B

BACK
Enlarge by 141% on a
photocopier and join
along dotted lines.

Cut 1 Pair

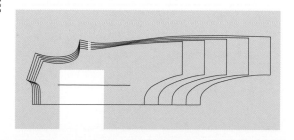

Onesie Version A+B

BACK
Enlarge by 141% on a
photocopier and join
along dotted lines.

Cut 1 Pair

2

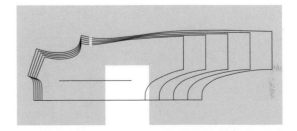

Onesie Version A+B

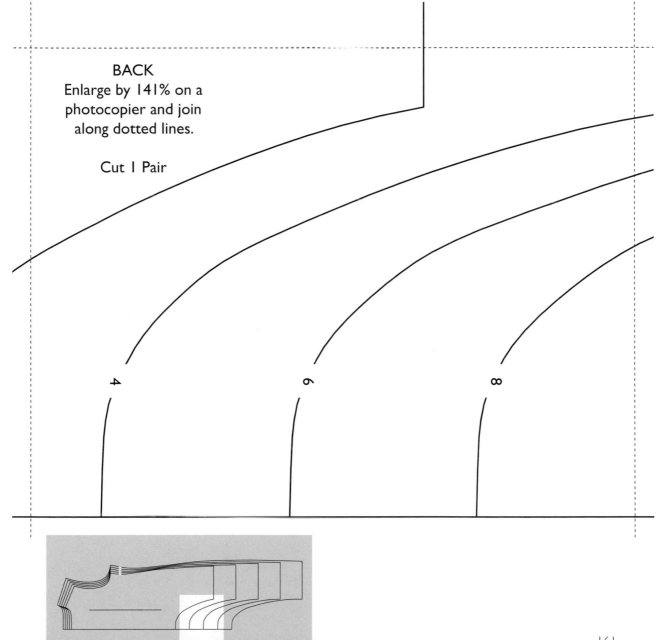

BACK
Enlarge by 141% on a
photocopier and join
along dotted lines.

Cut 1 Pair

4

6

8

Onesie Version A+B

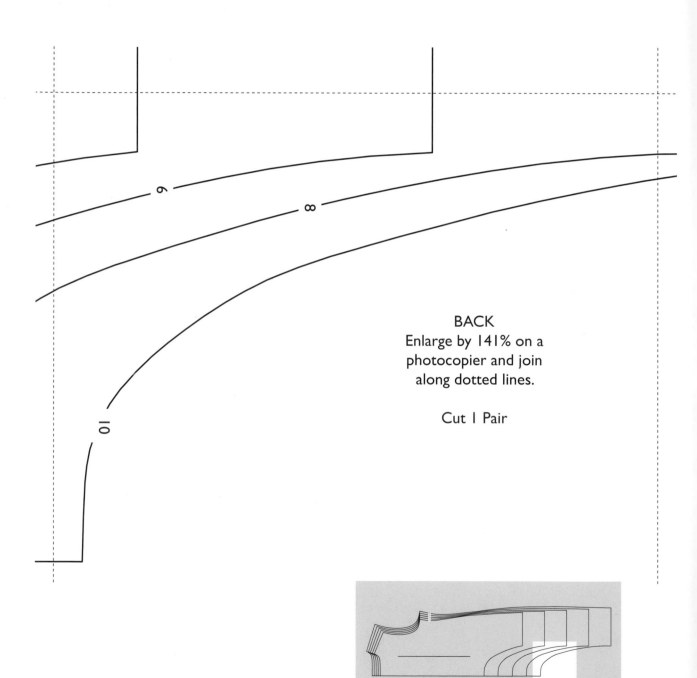

6

8

10

BACK
Enlarge by 141% on a
photocopier and join
along dotted lines.

Cut 1 Pair

Onesie Version A+B

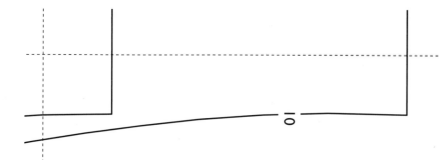

BACK
Enlarge by 141% on a
photocopier and join
along dotted lines.

Cut 1 Pair

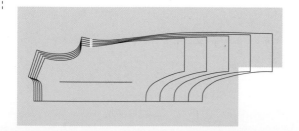

Dog

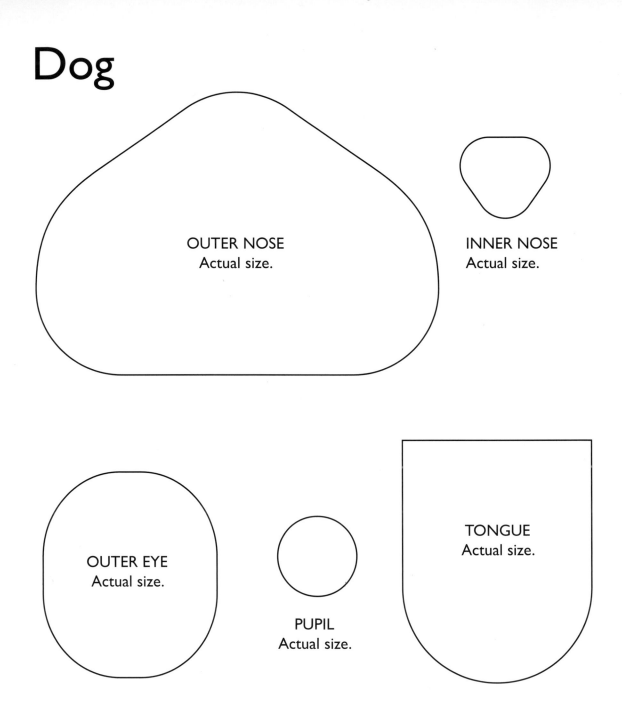

OUTER NOSE
Actual size.

INNER NOSE
Actual size.

OUTER EYE
Actual size.

PUPIL
Actual size.

TONGUE
Actual size.

Dog

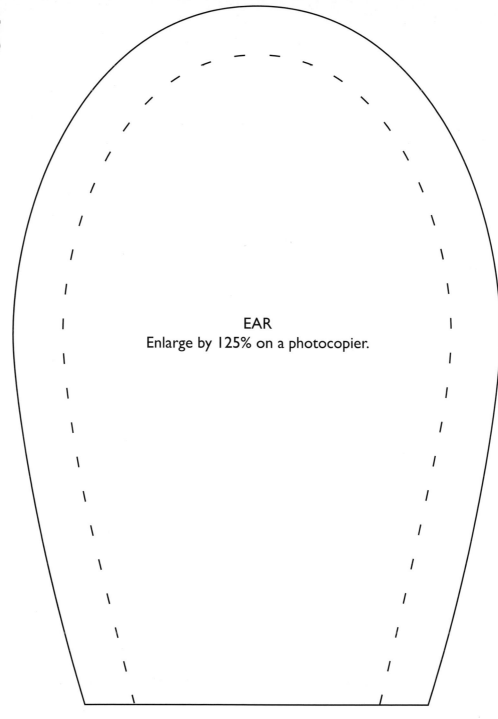

EAR
Enlarge by 125% on a photocopier.

Cat

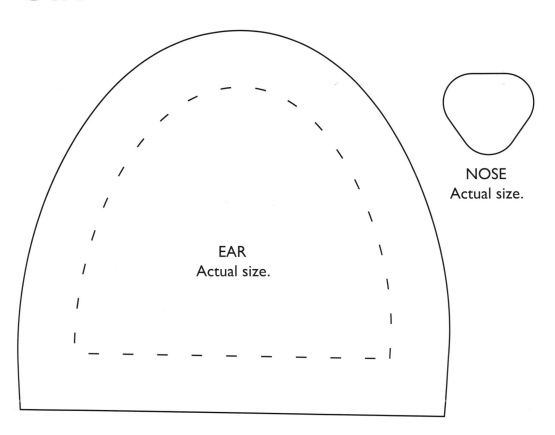

NOSE
Actual size.

EAR
Actual size.

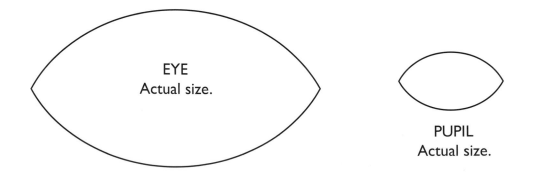

EYE
Actual size.

PUPIL
Actual size.

Tiger

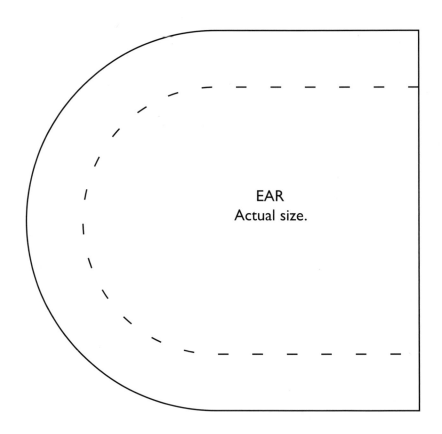

EAR
Actual size.

Reindeer

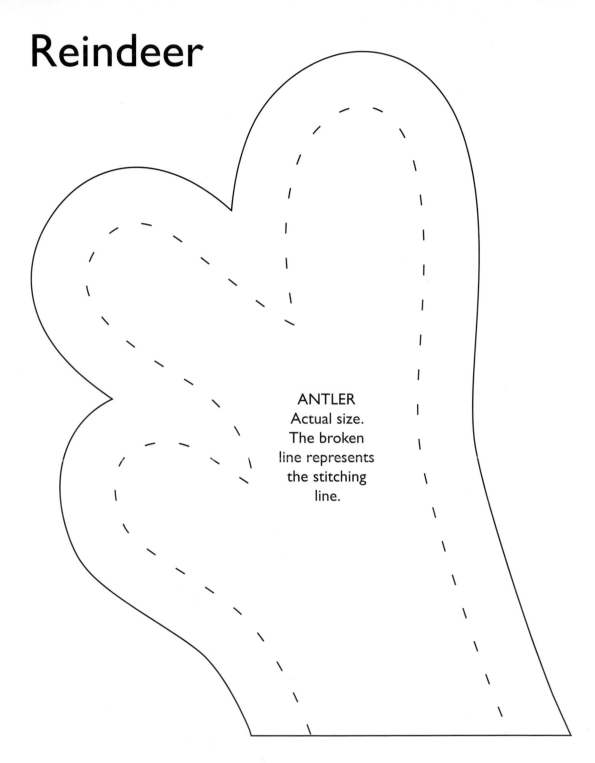

ANTLER
Actual size.
The broken
line represents
the stitching
line.

Reindeer

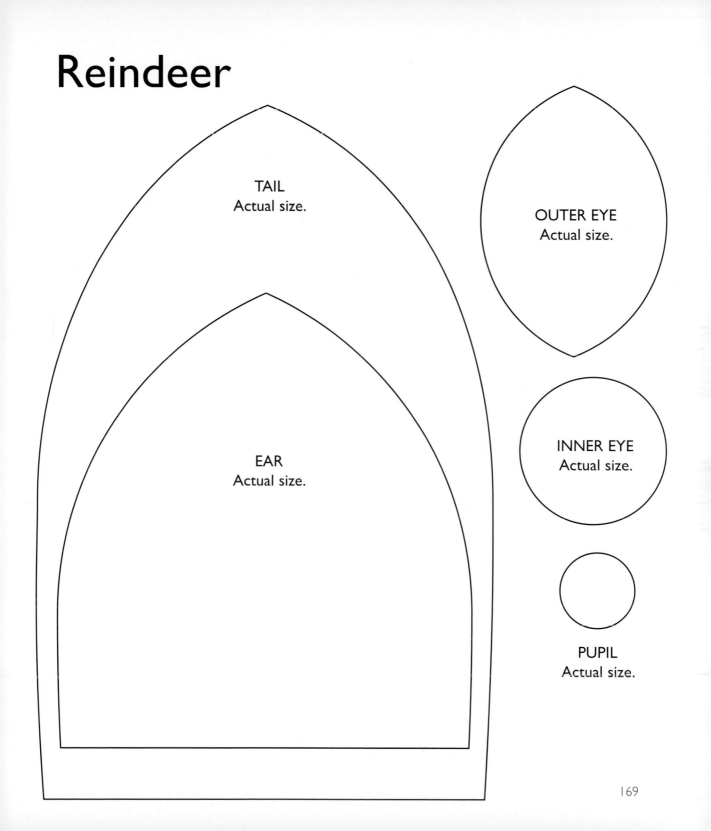

TAIL
Actual size.

OUTER EYE
Actual size.

INNER EYE
Actual size.

EAR
Actual size.

PUPIL
Actual size.

Elf

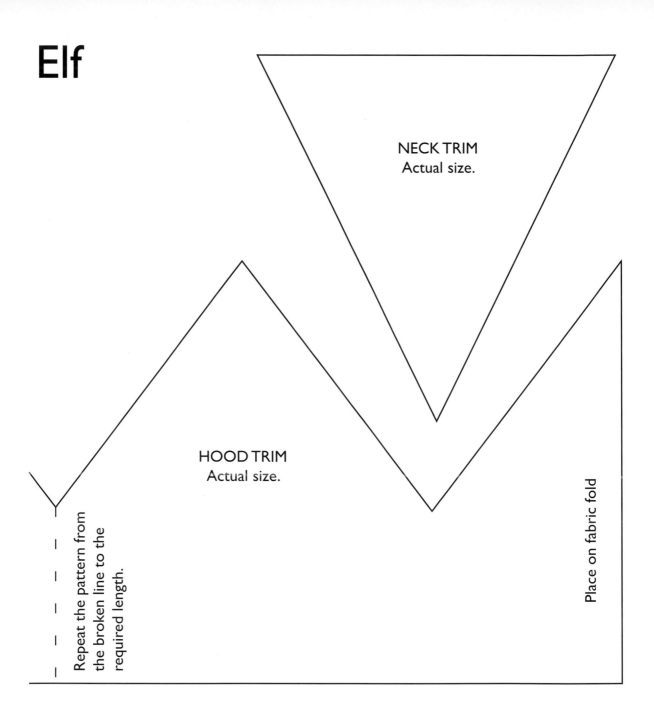

NECK TRIM
Actual size.

HOOD TRIM
Actual size.

Repeat the pattern from the broken line to the required length.

Place on fabric fold

Cow

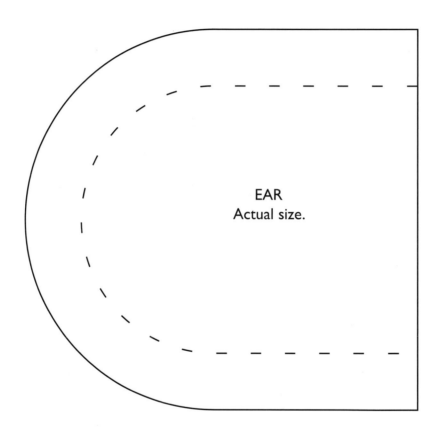

EAR
Actual size.

Duck

PUPIL
Actual size.

OUTER EYE
Actual size.

INNER EYE
Actual size.

HEAD COMB
Actual size.

The broken line
represents the
stitching line.

Duck

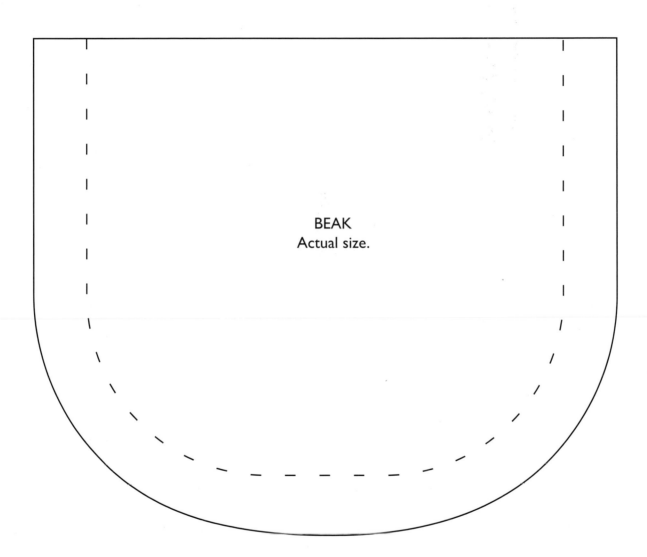

BEAK
Actual size.

Duck

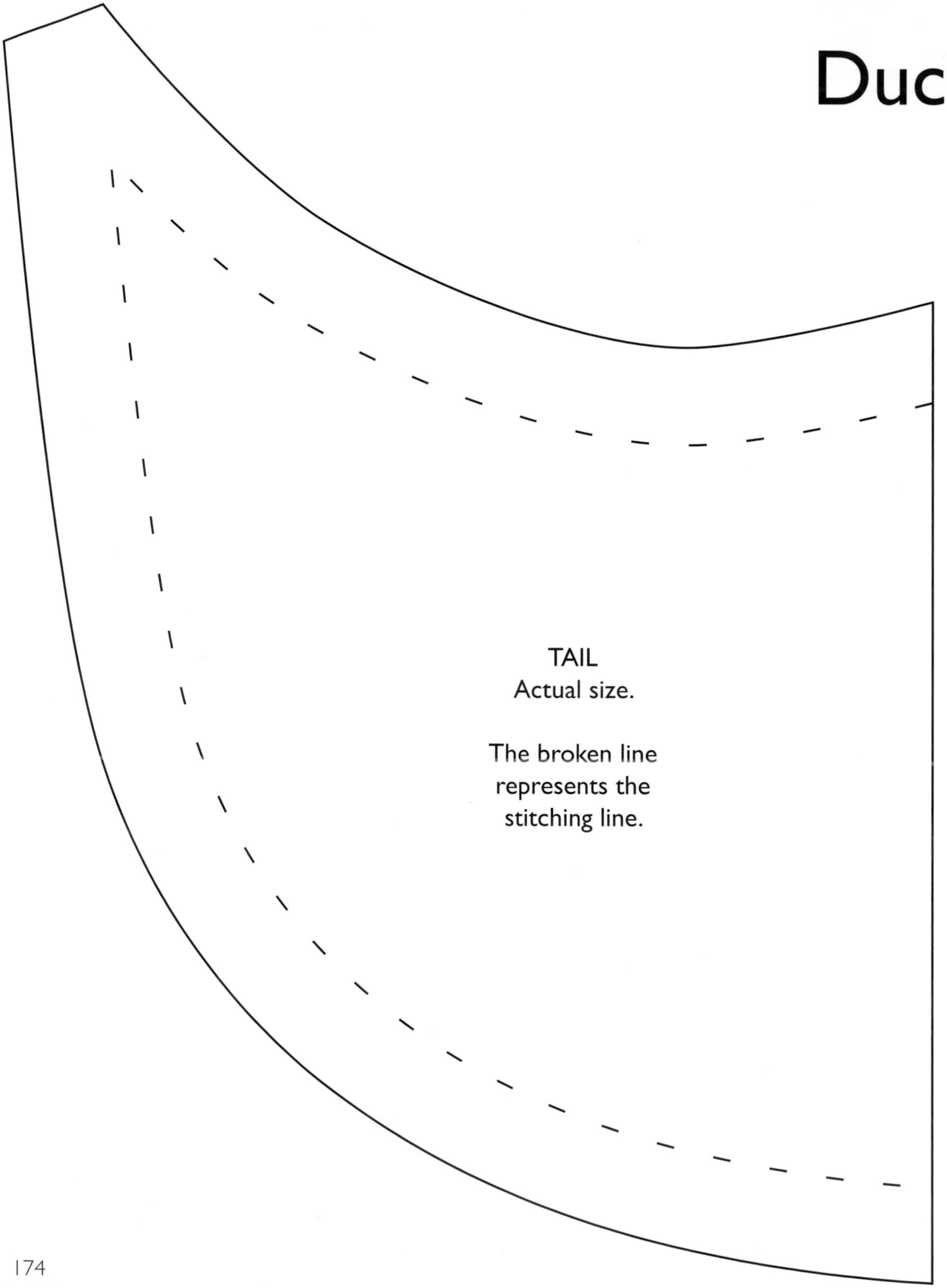

TAIL
Actual size.

The broken line
represents the
stitching line.

Pig

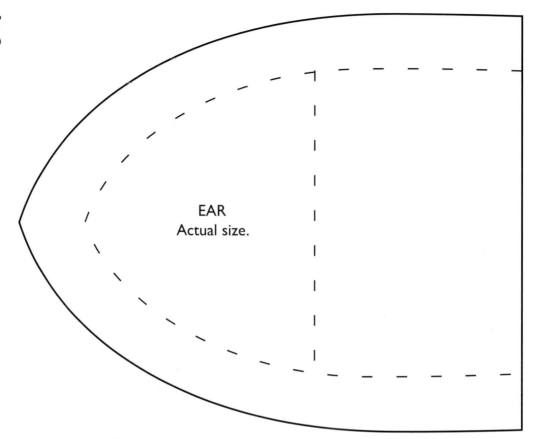

EAR
Actual size.

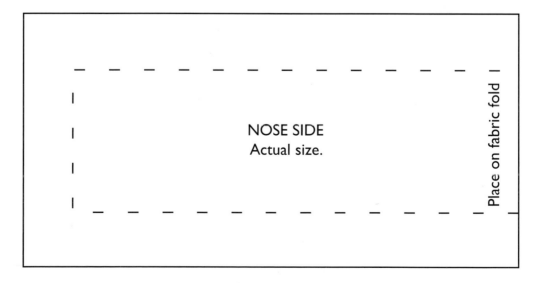

NOSE SIDE
Actual size.

Place on fabric fold

Pig

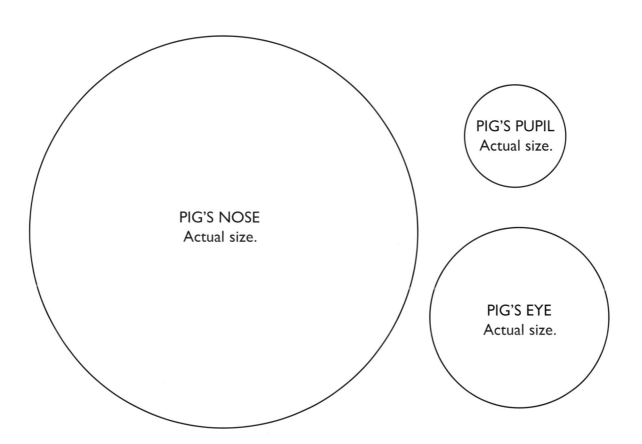

PIG'S NOSE
Actual size.

PIG'S PUPIL
Actual size.

PIG'S EYE
Actual size.

Monkey

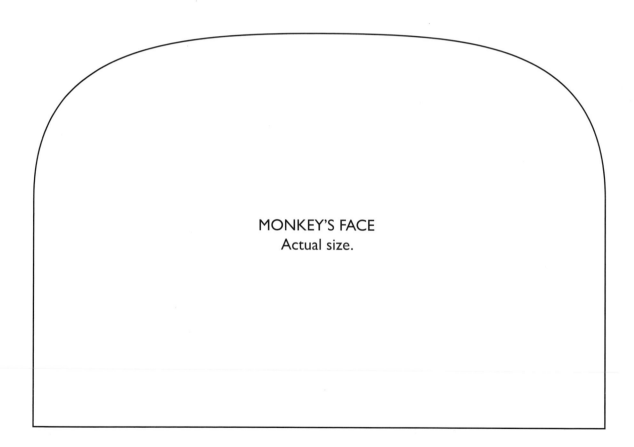

MONKEY'S FACE
Actual size.

Monkey

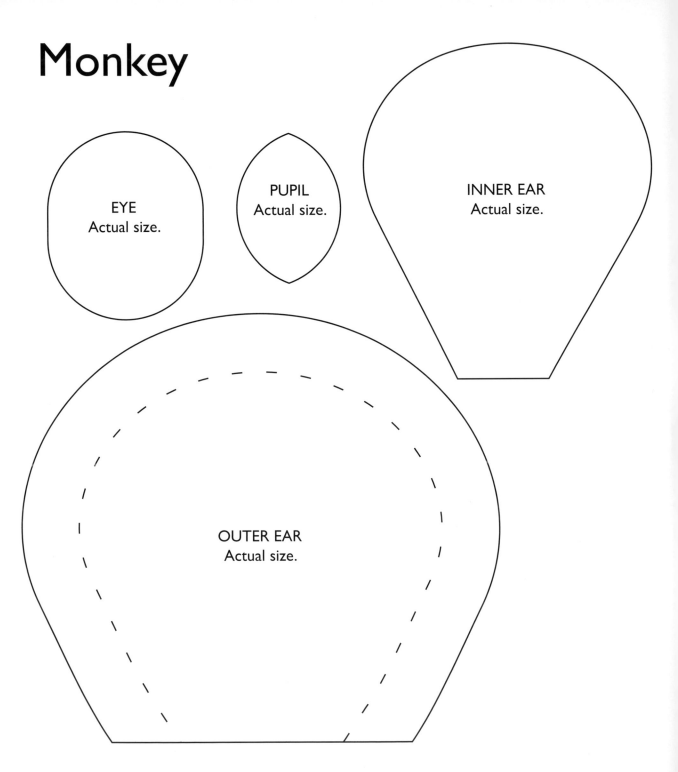

EYE
Actual size.

PUPIL
Actual size.

INNER EAR
Actual size.

OUTER EAR
Actual size.

Bunny

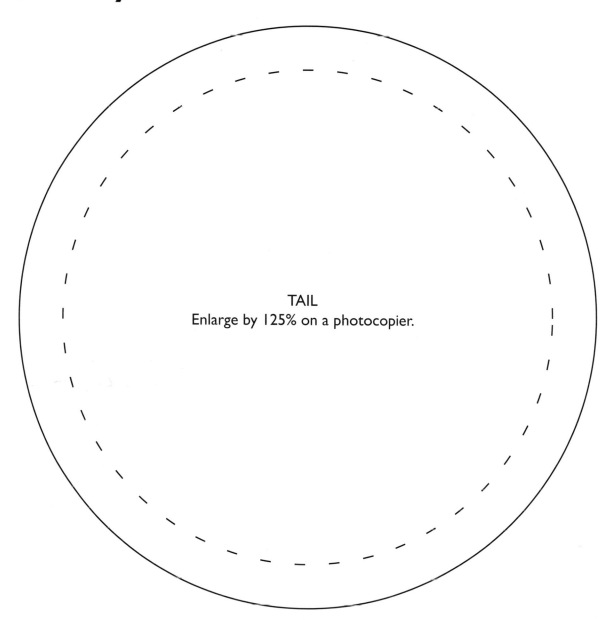

TAIL
Enlarge by 125% on a photocopier.

Bunny

PUPIL
Actual size.

EYE
Actual size.

TEETH
Actual size.

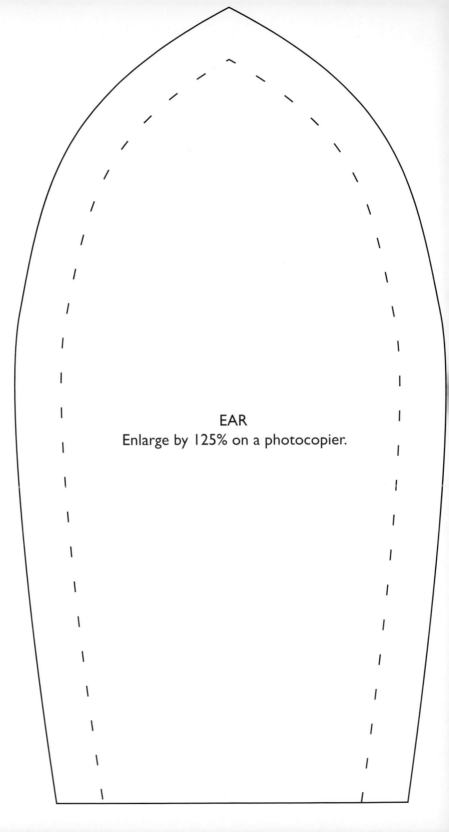

EAR
Enlarge by 125% on a photocopier.

Dinosaur

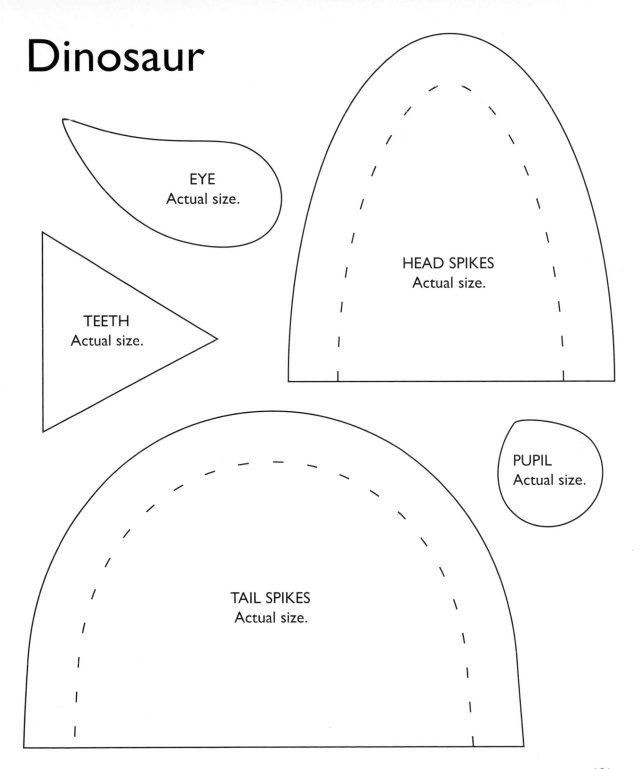

EYE
Actual size.

HEAD SPIKES
Actual size.

TEETH
Actual size.

PUPIL
Actual size.

TAIL SPIKES
Actual size.

Dinosaur

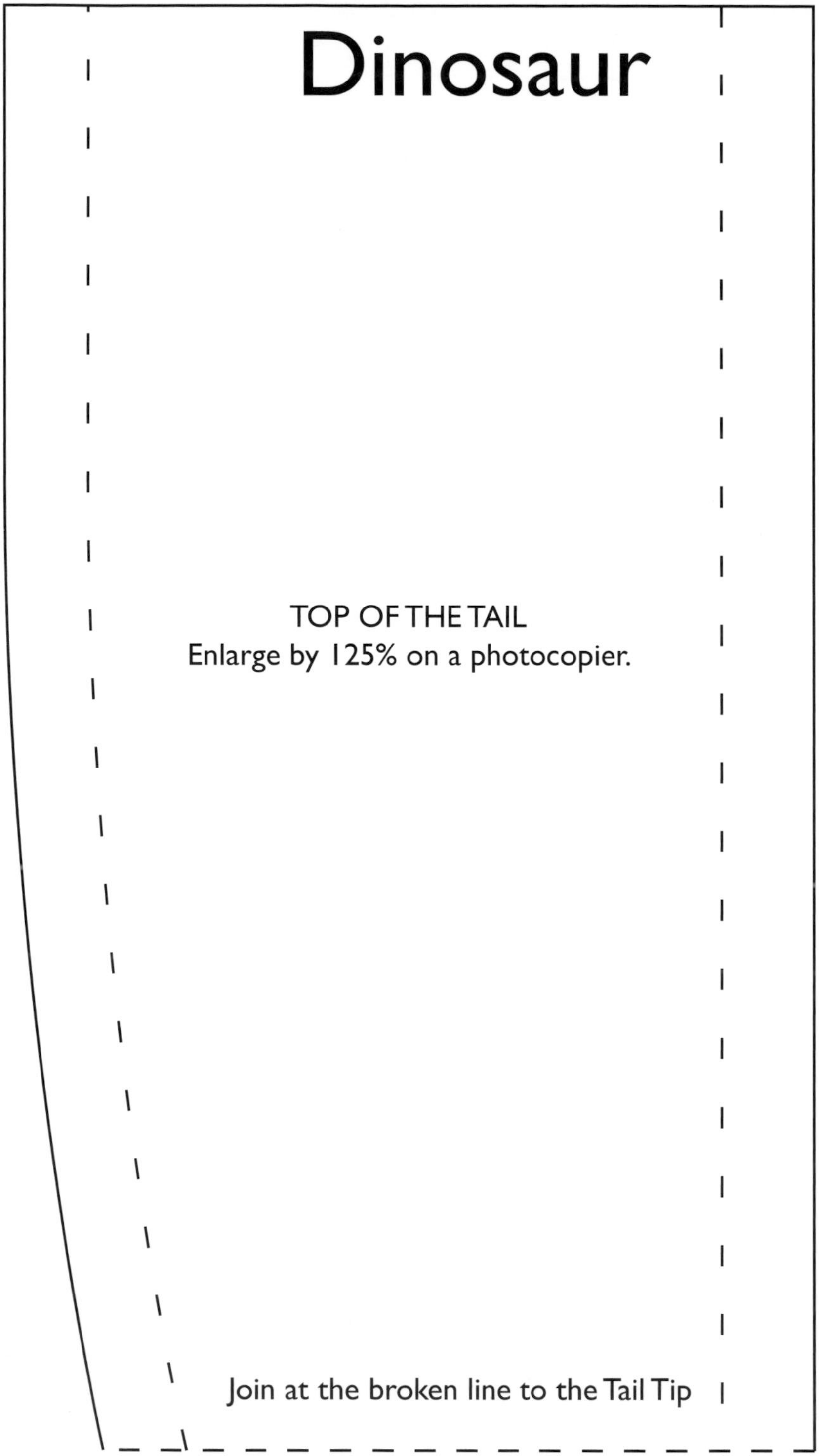

TOP OF THE TAIL
Enlarge by 125% on a photocopier.

Join at the broken line to the Tail Tip

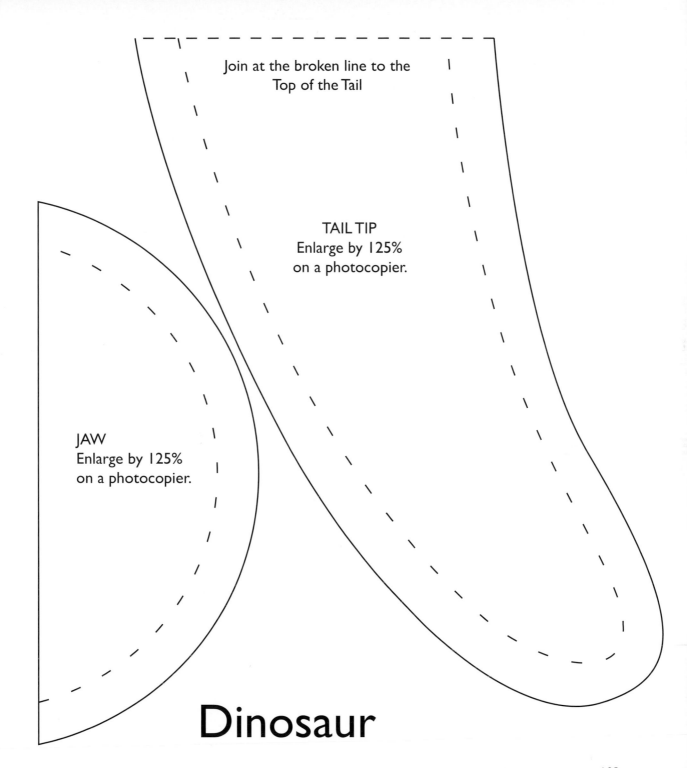

Join at the broken line to the
Top of the Tail

TAIL TIP
Enlarge by 125%
on a photocopier.

JAW
Enlarge by 125%
on a photocopier.

Dinosaur

Leopard

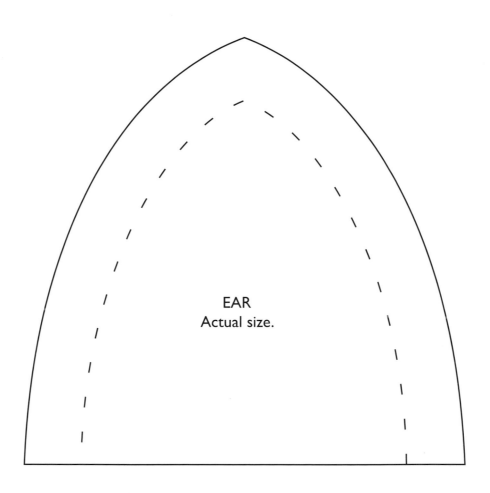

EAR
Actual size.

Pirate

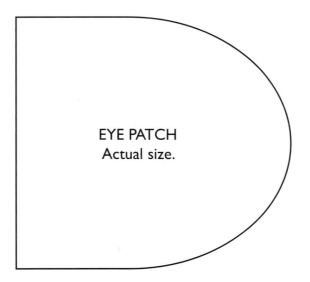

EYE PATCH
Actual size.

Pirate

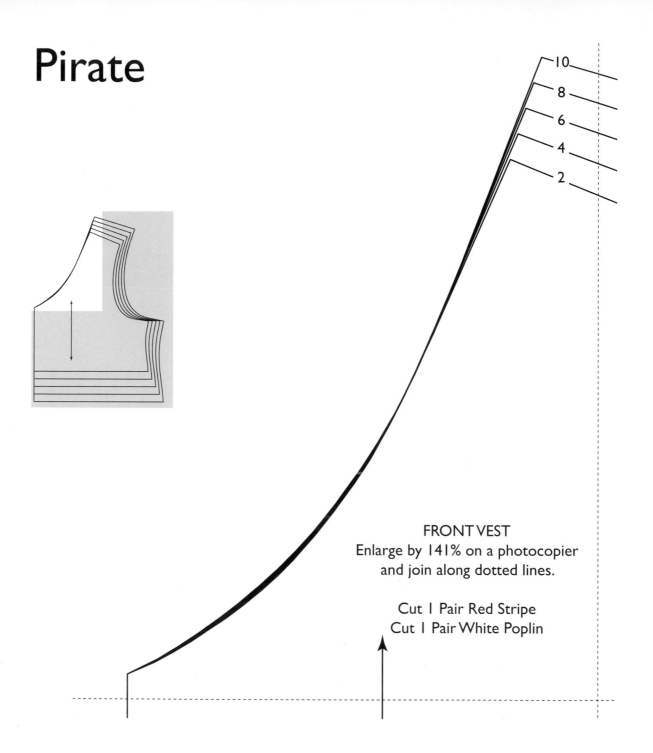

10

8

6

4

2

FRONT VEST
Enlarge by 141% on a photocopier
and join along dotted lines.

Cut 1 Pair Red Stripe
Cut 1 Pair White Poplin

Pirate

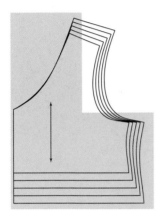

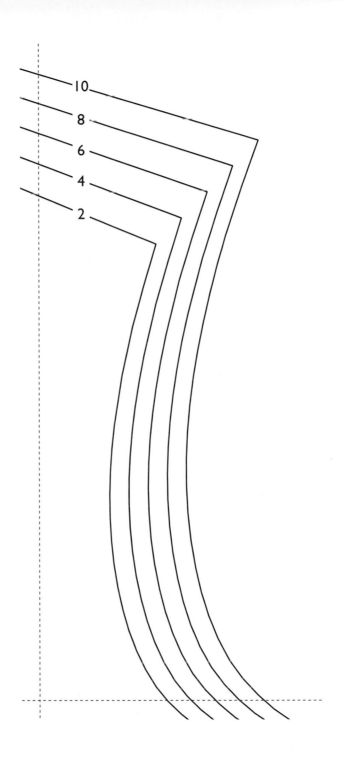

10

8

6

4

2

FRONT VEST
Enlarge by 141% on a photocopier
and join along dotted lines.

Cut 1 Pair Red Stripe
Cut 1 Pair White Poplin

Pirate

FRONT VEST
Enlarge by 141% on a photocopier
and join along dotted lines.

Cut 1 Pair Red Stripe
Cut 1 Pair White Poplin

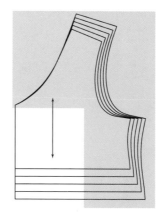

2

4

6

8

10

Pirate

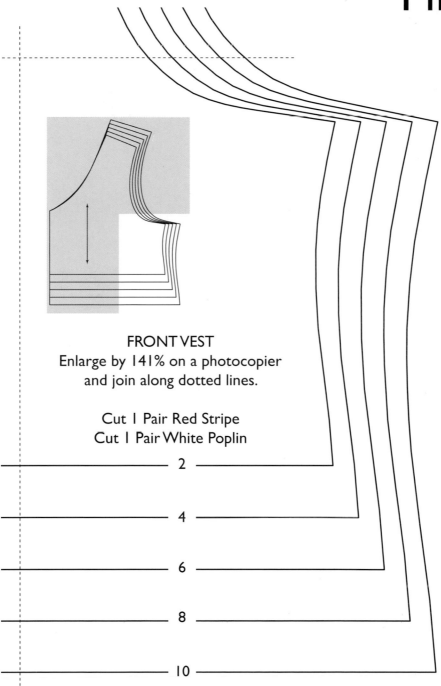

FRONT VEST
Enlarge by 141% on a photocopier
and join along dotted lines.

Cut 1 Pair Red Stripe
Cut 1 Pair White Poplin

2

4

6

8

10

Lady Beetle

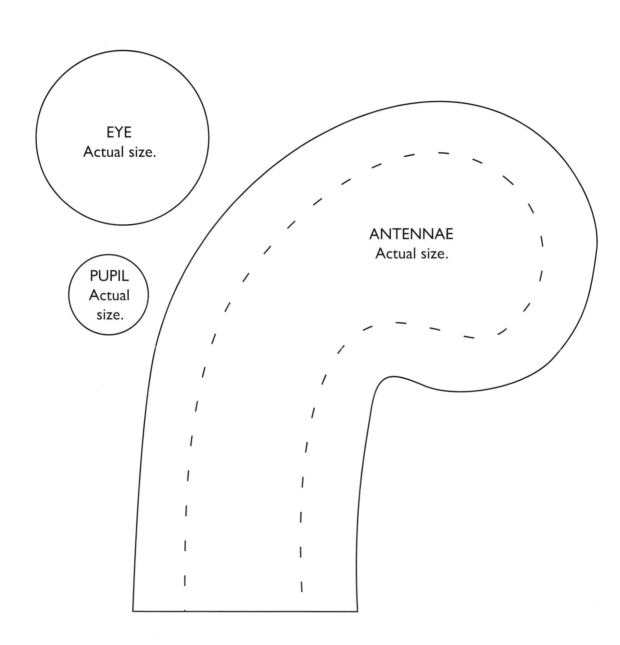

EYE
Actual size.

PUPIL
Actual
size.

ANTENNAE
Actual size.

Zebra

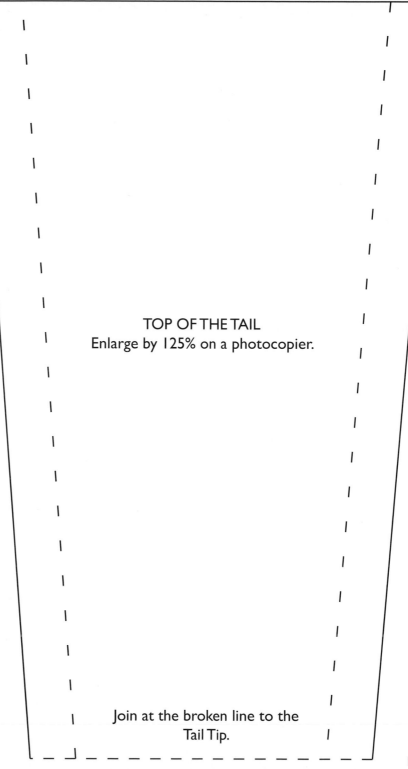

TOP OF THE TAIL
Enlarge by 125% on a photocopier.

Join at the broken line to the
Tail Tip.

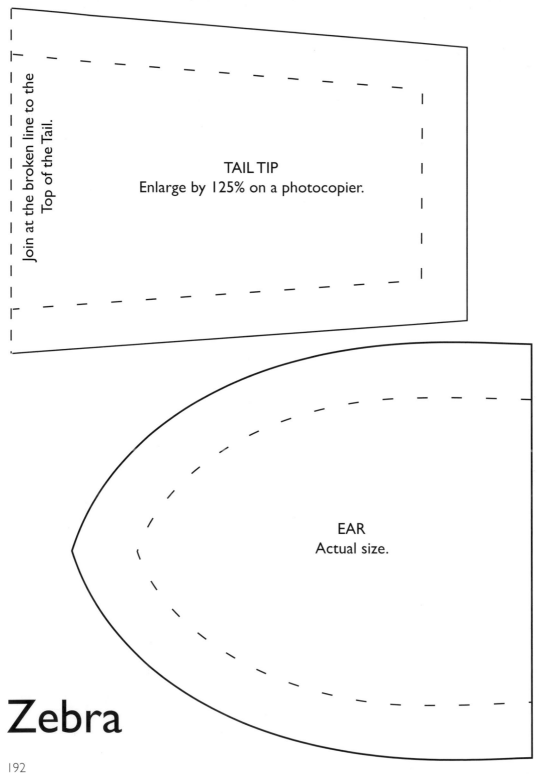

Join at the broken line to the Top of the Tail.

TAIL TIP
Enlarge by 125% on a photocopier.

EAR
Actual size.

Zebra

Elephant

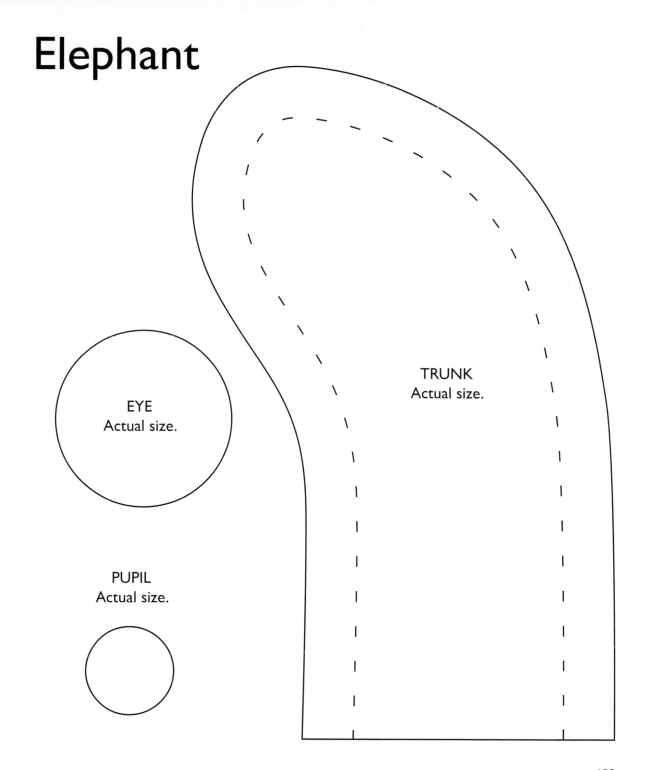

EYE
Actual size.

PUPIL
Actual size.

TRUNK
Actual size.

Elephant

EAR
Enlarge by 125% on a photocopier.

Elephant

Join at the broken line to the Tail Tip.

TOP OF THE TAIL
Enlarge by 125% on a photocopier.

Join at the broken line to the Top of the Tail.

TAIL TIP
Enlarge by 125% on a photocopier.

Giraffe

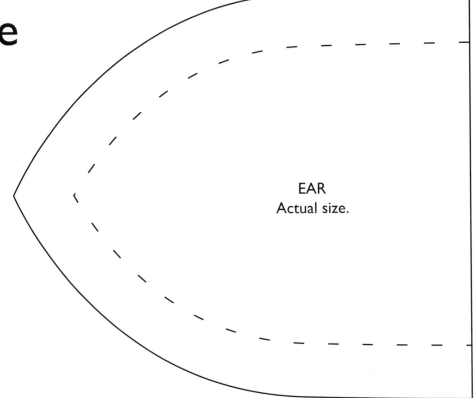

EAR
Actual size.

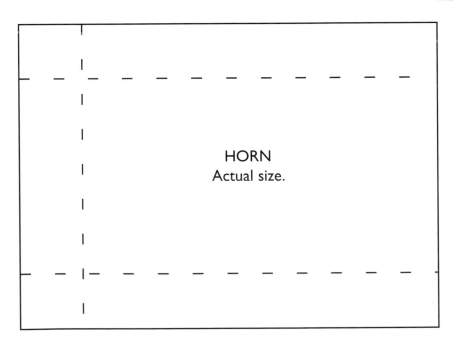

HORN
Actual size.

Giraffe

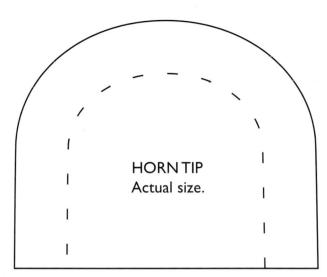

HORN TIP
Actual size.

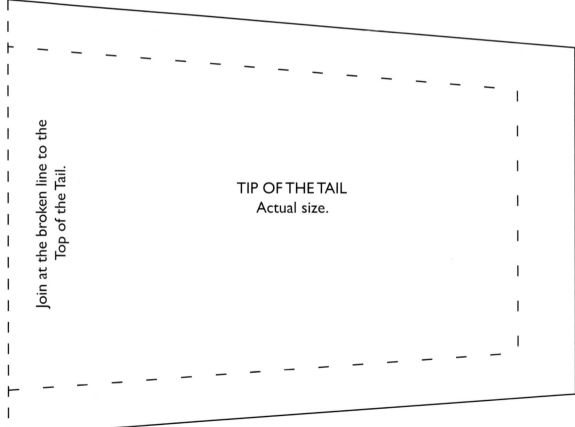

TIP OF THE TAIL
Actual size.

Join at the broken line to the Top of the Tail.

Giraffe

TOP OF THE TAIL
Enlarge by 125% on a photocopier.

Join at the broken line to the
Tip of the Tail.

Superhero

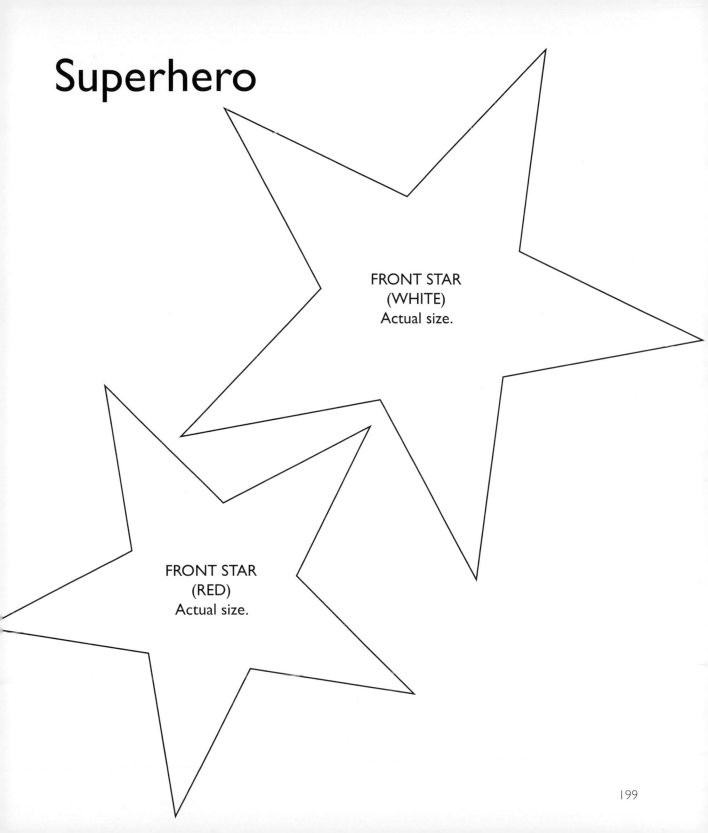

FRONT STAR
(WHITE)
Actual size.

FRONT STAR
(RED)
Actual size.

Superhero

BACK STAR (CAPE)
Enlarge by 125% on a photocopier.

Heart

HEART POCKET
Actual size.

Heart

BACK HEART
Enlarge by 125% on a
photocopier.

Place on fabric fold

Acknowledgements

I cannot imagine this book being possible without the support and patience of my wonderful family. Thank you to my husband, Darren, for believing in me always, and my son Ethan for reassuring me with his encouraging words: "Mum, its great...relax!"

I especially want to thank my daughter Ruby for being amazing, helpful and patient. Ruby has been my fit model, my design assistant and my creative companion. Ruby, you really are a gem.

A special thank you to my Mum and Dad for being my biggest fans.

A huge thank you to my friend Nicky for her fantastic photography and offering to be my assistant on any overseas publicity trips that I might happen to do!

Deborah Segaert, thank you for offering valuable advice, creative input and a much-needed chat.

I also want to thank Diane Ward for having such faith in me.

Thank you to the wonderful children who were happily photographed in the very warm Onesies regardless of the scorching hot day.

Thank you, finally, to all of my dear friends for happily listening to me rave on about this book, and yes, you can have my signature now!

This edition was published in 2015 by New Holland Publishers Pty Ltd
London • Sydney • Auckland

The Chandlery Unit 009, 50 Westminster Bridge Road London SE1 7QY United Kingdom
1/66 Gibbes Street Chatswood NSW 2067 Australia
5/39 Woodside Ave Northcote Auckland 0627 New Zealand

www.newhollandpublishers.com

A record of this book is held at the National Library of Australia.

ISBN: 9781742575674

Managing Director: Fiona Schultz
Publisher: Diane Ward
Editor: Simona Hill
Designer: Andrew Davies
Photography: Samantha Mackie
Production Director: Olga Dementiev
Printer: Toppan Leefung Printing Ltd (China)

10 9 8 7 6 5 4 3 2

Keep up with New Holland Publishers on Facebook
www.facebook.com/NewHollandPublishers